Emotional Self Mastery

Emotional Self Mastery

How to Be your Best

Simon Casey

Copyright © 2024 by Simon Casey.

ISBN: 9798890903358 (sc)
ISBN: 9798890903365 (e)

All rights reserved. No part of this book may be reproduced or transmitted in any form or by any means, electronic or mechanical, including photocopying, recording, or by any information storage and retrieval system, without permission in writing from the copyright owner.

The views expressed in this work are solely those of the author and do not necessarily reflect the views of the publisher, and the publisher hereby disclaims any responsibility for them.

EXPRESSO Executive Center 777, Dunsmuir Street Vancouver, BC V71K4
1-888-721-0662 ext 101
info@expressopublishing.com

Contents

Acknowledgments 9

Chapter 1	Journey To Emotional Self Mastery...............	11
Chapter 2	Who Is In Charge?..	15
	Physical Body	18
	Emotional Body	20
	Spiritual Body	23
Chapter 3	Emotional Intelligence	29
	Healthy, Functional Human Being	32
	Emotional Safety	34
	Positive Vs. Negative Feelings	36
Chapter 4	Emotional Self Mastery	39
	Feelings Vs. Emotions	41
	Identifying True Feelings	43
Chapter 5	Feelings	47
	Happy	50
	Fear	51
	Sad	51
	Hurt	52
	Anger	52
	Guilt	53
	Depression	53
Chapter 6	Understanding Core Feelings	57
	Happy	58
	Fear	62
	Sad	69
	Hurt	70
	Anger	74
	Guilt	79
Chapter 7	Stress And Depression	83
	Stress	83

Chapter 8	Depression	85
	How To Process Feelings	89
	Magical Thinking	95
	Trust Your Intuition Or "Gut Feelings"	95
	Road Blocks To Emotional Self Mastery	96
	Emotional Vs. Emotionless	106
	Resistance To Change	107
	Defenses—The Illusion Of Self-Protection	108
Chapter 9	Relationships	111
Chapter 10	Coming To Terms With Our Past	119
	Processing Old Resentments	122
	Forgiveness	127
Chapter 11	Belief FActor	131
	What Are Beliefs?	133
	Cycle Of Negative Belief Formation	134
	Emotional Beliefs	136
	Brain Vs. Mind	138
	Conscious Mind Vs. Subconscious Mind	139
	Shame And Toxic Shame	142
	Change Your Beliefs, Change Your World	146
	Psych-K	147
	Is There A Light At The End Of The Tunnel?	149
	Love	151
	Integrity	153
	Your Purpose	155
Appendix A	Emotional Intelligence Test	159
	Eiq Test	159
Index		173

Acknowledgments

I would like to thank all of the people who took part in creating this book for their never-ending love and encouragement. This includes Kelly Frey, for being a wonderful editor who is generous and kind, for putting in many long hours of hard work, and for putting up with my continuous desire to write more—I am forever grateful. I also want to thank my mom for loving me and making me feel very special and for teaching me how to share my gift with those who have come into my life and have chosen to take this wild ride with me.

I hope this book will bring some insight and healing for those who are suffering and guidance for those who seek a meaningful life.

CHAPTER 1

Journey to Emotional Self Mastery

> *If you are distressed by anything external or internal, the pain is not due to the thing itself, but to your estimate of it; And this you have the power to revoke at any moment.*
>
> —Marcus Aurelius, 167 ACE

Imagine your life without any regrets. What would that be like? When you look in the mirror, do you like what you see? Do you accept yourself, as you are, unconditionally?

We are all human and therefore imperfect. We all have weaknesses. In our younger years, our insecurities make it difficult for us to accept these weaknesses and therefore very resistant to positive criticism or suggestions for self-improvement. We defend. We deny. It becomes a way of life. But as we grow older, and our bodies begin to age, we are confronted with many things that we can no longer ignore. It becomes harder to lose weight. The mirror becomes less and less kind. As our defenses start crumbling slowly like an old Roman building, revealing our weaknesses, fears, secrets, resentments, and regrets, inevitably the real truth about our hidden self is revealed. It becomes evident that our perception of our ego, or who we thought we were, is no longer the case. Eventually we come face-to-face with what we have been avoiding for decades—our true selves. By avoiding our true selves throughout the majority of our lives, we only postpone the inevitable.

Older people tend to be much more content and honest than younger people. Why is that? The reason has to do with acceptance. In our elder years, as we're faced with our weaknesses and a more realistic view of our place in the world, we find peace and with peace comes freedom instead of regret.

There's no need to wait for our senior years to find peace. Life can be so much happier, and infinitely more fulfilling, from the moment we learn to truly understand ourselves. To do this requires identifying and embracing our limitations and shortcomings. Only then can we experience the pure joy that comes from seeing, accepting, and loving ourselves as we truly are.

But learning to accept our true selves is not as easy as it sounds. And the exercise can be painful. So why bother? Because it's difficult to love someone who doesn't accept themselves. Those of us who deny our true selves have a propensity to take out our shortcomings on others. So do it for those who love you. But more importantly, do it for you. You deserve it.

> *If your life feels empty because you are still wondering what to give to it, if you are emotionally bankrupt, you already made your decision.*

We are the creators of our own reality, and that reality is based on our feelings. Our reality is the way we perceive our past, our present, and our future. It's the way we connect to our highest (spiritual) self and make some sense out of life. While we each process information differently, the way we experience feelings, whether anger, hurt, pleasure or fear, is essentially the same.

Feelings are the conscious result of the interaction between the cerebral cortex, or "thinking" part of the brain, the limbic system, or "feeling" part of the brain, and the internal organs, all of which together produce changes that affect not only the brain, but the whole body. Our emotional responses, however, are also the product of first—and secondhand knowledge. Secondhand knowledge is that which we learn from someone else's experiences, while firsthand knowledge is that which we come to know through our own discovery and experiences. While feelings are part of firsthand knowledge, they are easily misunderstood. If we don't understand our feelings, we cannot truly understand ourselves, and confusion and conflict become our reality. Only through accurately understanding our feelings can we learn to free ourselves from negative emotions, which provides more creative energy, as well as the opportunity for limitless personal growth, and, ultimately, connects us to our higher selves.

Unfortunately, many of us are not interested in self-examination and are unwilling to embark on a soul-searching journey toward our true potential. Many of us believe our lives are already good enough or that we don't deserve better. Sadly, many of us often live our lives like high-functioning zombies, out of touch with our true selves and our feelings.

> *You can choose to be emotionally wealthy or emotionally bankrupt, but the amount of work is still the same.*

We are each responsible for our own lives and for the degree to which we pursue our life's purpose. Deciding to focus on personal growth and enlightenment may be perceived by others as selfish. But we cannot reach our full potential without taking the time to focus on ourselves. Achieving emotional self mastery requires the desire and the willingness to understand our feelings and belief systems and the courage to do the work to transform into the best possible person that we can be. There is nothing wrong with this self-interest; in fact, it is the ultimate expression of respect for our humanity. In the words of Ayn Rand, "Man—every man—is an end in himself, not a means to the ends of others; he must live for his own sake, neither sacrificing himself to others nor sacrificing others to himself; he must work for his rational self-interest, with the achievement of his own happiness as the highest moral purpose of his life."[11]

To progress on our journey toward self-discovery, we must break down our resistance. We can accomplish this through a better understanding of what makes each of us a better person as we become more centered. When we are centered within, we draw strength to channel our creative energy by aligning our actions/reactions (physical body), our feelings/behaviors (emotional body), and our purpose (spiritual body) without being ego-driven.

I hope that this book will open your heart, enlighten your mind, and bring love and peace in your soul.

Socrates believed that "an unexamined life is not worth living," and I believe that "your clarity will define you at the end."

---

[1] Rand, A. (1962). *Introducing Objectivism*. Retrieved from http://www.aynrand.org/site/PageServer?page-name=objectivism_intro.

CHAPTER 2 — *Who Is In Charge?*

> *If you want to know what your body will look like in the future, examine your mind today. If you want to know what your mind was like in the past, examine your body today*
>
> —Casey

From the moment we enter the world, our senses reassure us that we live in a physical world. The powerful reassurance of sight, sound, and smell constantly reinforce our physical nature while ignoring the other elements due to the limitations of our senses. Because of this, it is nearly impossible for us to evolve as complete beings. Hence most of us focus on our physical manifestation in this world, our physical body, seldom viewing ourselves as a composition of several parts that make us a whole person. We get lost in the materialism of this physical world. At some point we may catch a glimpse of ourselves from a different level of consciousness and begin to understand the unique parts of our being and how they together create wholeness.

The mind-body connection is an undeniable truth. But many times we resist understanding the importance of this relationship. To progress on our journey toward self-discovery, we must break down such resistance. We can accomplish this through a better understanding of what makes each of us a whole person. The realization that we are more than just one body is the first step toward higher consciousness. But most importantly, our day-to-day experience confirms this reality.

There are three core elements of our being:

- Physical Body—Primarily interested in our survival and materialism
- Emotional Body—Our personal experiences and our reaction to the world
- Spiritual Body—Divine force or energy; connection to our highest self

The way in which we come to terms with our feelings and beliefs and our reactions to our environment eventually determine which body type we avoid and which we embrace as a dominant factor in our lives. Ultimately the kinds of relationships, jobs, and so on we choose directly correlate to how we internalize these elements.

Our senses dominate our perceptions from very early on, and the resulting beliefs persuade us to become more physical-body oriented. Not surprisingly, materialism becomes the driving force of the physical body as it constantly reinforces our ego (who we think we are) and our false sense of self-worth. Greed and excess do not satisfy the insatiable ego—we are always left wanting more. Without realizing it, as we become more physical-body dominant, we become disconnected, with limited understanding of who we are in our core being.

As we get older, we become dominated by one, or occasionally two, of the three bodies. For instance, if we are more physical-body oriented, we may be fixated on how we look, keeping our body in shape, even having plastic surgeries to enhance our physical appearance. If we are more emotional-body oriented, we may be preoccupied with emotional self-improvement, reading an endless stream of self-help books and attending self-help seminars or establishing relationships in which we feel victimized. If we are spiritual-body oriented, we may place an inordinate amount of emphasis on religion, constantly searching for a spiritual guru or other spiritual enlightenment.

You may think at first glance that the physical body is least important. Others may argue that the spiritual body is least important. This is a mistake. All three elements are irrevocably intertwined, each affecting the other. Consider these examples:

You come home from dinner at a restaurant and, to your dismay, realize you have food poisoning. Your husband is in a romantic mood; you couldn't be less interested. You try to pray as usual before going to sleep, but you can't even concentrate on that. Your physical body is in full revolt, superseding all other aspects of your being.

You are depressed. You feel as if you have nothing to look forward to. Your emotional body is in pain. You can hardly find the energy to get out of bed in the morning, much less even consider driving all the way to the gym to work out. You feel as if gravity is pulling extra hard on your body. Your physical body is exhausted. You know intellectually you should meditate or pray or do something to pull yourself out of this funk, but you feel as if life has no meaning, so what's the point? Plus you don't have the energy anyway.

You are at a cocktail party and the conversation turns to mental illness. One of the guests has a brother who lives in a state hospital, suffering from schizophrenia. Another guest asks the first guest if he ever hopes God just takes his brother, rescuing him from a life of misery. The first guest gets angry, telling the second guest that we all have a purpose on Earth even those with extraordinary challenges. An argument ensues. You watch this exchange feeling as if you are on another planet. You are a bit intrigued by the passion the two guests have about the subject of religion but cannot grasp how they might have developed such convictions. In fact, you can't really even imagine what it would be like to have a mentally ill family member. In addition to having no sense of spirituality, you are emotionally numb. You are a bystander, watching life go by, but not really participating. You view life as just a series of days, and then one day it is over. That's why you let yourself go physically—what's the point in trying to extend such a life?

The point is, to achieve emotional wellness; we must understand all three components of our being and learn to bring them into a balance.

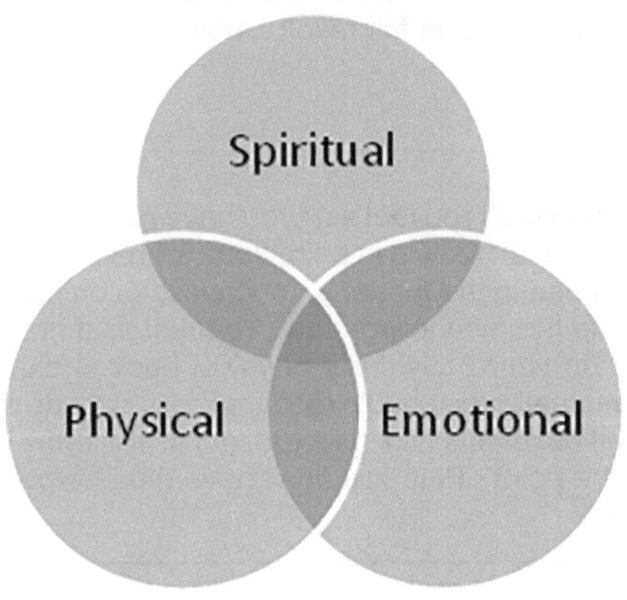

Physical body

The physical body needs no introduction. It is the outer you, the part that is obvious to all. It is the basis of our experience in the world and of fundamental importance in human life. Our physical body provides a sense of separation and individuality. Based upon our senses, we can't deny the existence of our physical body. Or can we?

We experience the world through our senses. Even though this input is very limited, our interpretation of this physical information shapes our understanding of the physical world. For example, the way a bat experiences the world is very different than a snake's experience. Because we are able to touch and feel things, we come to believe that we are mostly a physical body, not realizing that our physical body is merely an experiencer—a messenger or vehicle.

Most importantly, our physical body is in constant communication with our spiritual and emotional bodies. When we neglect our physical body and become ill, both our emotional and spiritual bodies also suffer. Even an illness as simple as a common cold impacts not only our physical body but our spiritual body as we have no energy to pray or otherwise connect with our highest self and emotionally we feel down. We couldn't care less about eating our favorite meal when we have a cold, and if we do, it tastes like cardboard. It's the exact same meal we love when we're healthy; what's the difference? Even though the body sends signals of starvation for food, loss of desire and feeling emotionally down make our favorite meal even less desirable and in some cases overrides the body's hunger signals to the point that we cannot eat. This is evident when we lose a loved one—the overwhelming pain overrides the body's need to eat or the ability to experience joy.

Consider our relationships with our cars. We depend on them to get us where we need to go. Some of us maintain our cars regularly so that they serve us for a long time. Others neglect the regular maintenance but regularly wash and polish the car so it always looks nice, then are shocked and angry when the car unexpectedly breaks down. Our bodies too are vehicles on which we rely to get us where we need to go. When we abuse or neglect our bodies, inevitably the body presents its bill in the form of chronic pain or disease. When this happens we become angry and resentful, wondering why this is happening to us. Our physical suffering brings us down emotionally, perhaps into depression, and our spiritual energy becomes stifled. Our body is a gift, but it's up to us how well we nurture it.

Emotional body

> *Experience is not what happens to you; it is what you do with what happens to you.*
> —Aldous Huxley

The term "emotional body" is hard to grasp at first. Not only do we seldom talk about it, but many of us do not even know that it exists. Emotions are invisible and yet have a profoundly powerful effect on us.

Every moment we are creating thoughts and having experiences, trying to make some sense of our world. Thoughts are powerful and measurable, just like emotions. For example, the military is developing new equipment to measure thoughts, and equipment already exists that enables a person to manipulate a video game with his thoughts by measuring the thoughts and translating them into action (this is called EEG neurofeedback).

Emotions can be measured as well. For example, shame emits a different frequency than guilt. Every emotion has its own vibration energy, similar to a tuning fork that, when struck, vibrates and puts out a certain energy frequency. When we are feeling intense emotions, our bodies vibrate at a different rate than when we are not. Therefore, we experience emotions through our physical body. However, most of us are not well connected to our physical body, meaning that we do not understand the emotional messages that are manifesting in it. Such disconnection makes us reactive rather than proactive, often looking for quick fixes and seeking instant gratification. For example, if we have a headache, we take aspirin, and if that doesn't relieve the pain, we see a doctor to get some prescription medication. But this approach merely masks the problem, and sooner or later our body presents its bill.

We are beings of energy; our thoughts and feelings are also energy. We are made of cells that are composed of atoms, which are nothing but energy. Our individual energy exists in balance, and any disruption of this balance negatively impacts our sense of physical and emotional well-being. If an emotion is strong enough, the body's energy field becomes overwhelmed, and the energy of that emotion becomes trapped in certain areas of the body (those that have a weakness, such as preexisting health condition). These repressed emotions have a huge impact on our physical body. They affect the tissues that are associated with the region of the body in which the energy is trapped, causing them to vibrate in tune with the trapped negative energy. The tissues literally feel that emotion on a continual basis, until it is released. Each of us is different as to where we hold these negative emotions. Depending on where we "hold" our emotions, the energy will manifest itself in that region. For example, unexpressed sadness may result in a lump in our throat; unexpressed tension may result in "butterflies" in our stomach; unexpressed grief may result in a physical pain in our heart. When we learn to experience and understand our emotional body as it is communicating with us through our physical body, we are able to stay grounded, balanced, and have the emotional ability to take care of ourselves.

Research has found that when a person was subjected to brief anger, his immune system was still depressed more than five hours later, and that as the anger was reconciled, the immune response increased for more than five hours after the conciliatory event (Ryan, Atkinson, and McCredy, 1995).1 This study clearly indicates the impact of negative emotions on the physical body. Imagine the impact of these trapped negative emotions on the body after six years . . . or sixteen years . . . or sixty years. It's time to consider the concept of disease and suffering as more than a coincidence; it is in fact often a phenomenon of our creation.

Physical Body ———— **Spiritual Body**

As the previous graphic illustrates, the emotional body is the bridge that provides the ultimate communication between our core being and our surface being. Imagine that you wish to have a baby. The feeling of joy and happiness at the thought of having a baby increasingly vibrates as it travels from your spiritual body through your emotional bridge to your physical body. Your physical body takes part by getting pregnant. At this news, the joyful feeling travels back toward the spiritual body, vibrating at an even higher frequency resulting in an almost euphoric feeling, ultimately reaching your spiritual body which rewards you at that moment with personal fulfillment. But what if that emotional bridge is collapsed or blocked by unresolved emotions which are now toxic? Your desire to have a baby cannot make it onto the bridge. You feel disconnected from yourself somehow and don't understand why. This creates another emotional roadblock. Each emotional barrier pushes the physical and spiritual bodies further apart.

Now let's assume you go to a seminar about how to create financial wealth. You have been feeling sad and depressed inside. As you participate the seminar, you realize that you have an inner desire to be wealthy. Your motivation is activated. You are forcing your brain to think positively, your body feels energized, and you feel as if you can conquer the world. But after you walk away from the seminar nothing much happens. The feeling of sadness or depression resurfaces and interferes with your desired goal. No amount of positive thinking, external motivation or mind-altering drugs will overcome the roadblock your emotional body is experiencing.

As our physical and spiritual bodies become further disconnected due to blockages in our emotional body that serve as roadblocks between the two, we become emotionally numb, callus and indifferent. We see everything through the lens of our physical body and the physical world. We become the servant of our own ego. Vanity becomes our best friend. We define ourselves with money, property and other things as we gradually lose ourselves to a life of pretense and false posturing, ultimately pronouncing ourselves happy.

Unfortunately, we are gradually evolving into a society of isolationism, narcissism, and emotional anemia. As we became more modernized, parenting styles started shifting gradually toward increased use of technology (e.g., video games, TV, cell phones). As the amount of time children spend with these devices increases at an alarming rate, it is inversely affecting their social skills. Being unable to interact and emotionally engage with others leads to children who are socially deprived. This inevitably presents significant consequences in adult relationships. No wonder text messaging is becoming the preferred communication method of the future—it doesn't require intimacy!

Spiritual body

The spiritual body, like the emotional body, is invisible and yet very real. However, the way it manifests itself differs from the emotional body. The spiritual body is experienced through love, compassion, and purpose, which are experienced in higher consciousness.

Our life experiences are like snowflakes. Each one is different. As each snowflake meets another, they form a unique shape, much like our experiences join together and begin to shape ourselves. At some point, the snow starts melting and turns into a creek, wildly running down the street, much like our preteen and teen years wrought with confusion and turmoil. As the creek becomes a river, it slows down and begins to create a meandering path, much as we slowdown in our middle years, having gained some wisdom, and start to shape our lives, beginning a journey of self-discovery. As the river finally merges into the ocean, it becomes one with its ultimate destiny. As we reach our later years we realize the wisdom of our higher purpose, waiting for us to merge, and in the end realize we were always a part of the whole.

Compassion helps us realize that we are all the same; we are all human. The ability to reach for others, to feel for them, to help them, and to be able to comfort them comes from our spiritual body. We don't consciously think about acting compassionately, weighing the emotional risk, instead, it's as if a unique self-inside of us has already made the decision without regard for the potential harm that may come to us as a result.

A few years ago at Kennedy airport in New York, a plane was unable to stop on the icy runway and plunged into the icy Hudson River. During the rescue effort, a chopper located a woman trying desperately to swim to stay alive. The rescue officer threw down the rope several times, but practically blind with exhaustion, the woman's attempts to grab the rope were unsuccessful. As hypothermia started setting in, the woman's movements slowed, and she started bobbing under the surface of the water. The rescue officer jumped into the icy water without any protection and saved her life. This example is no different than a mother running into a burning house to save her children.

Life without purpose has no meaning, no direction, and no enlightenment. As we discover our natural talents and gifts, and consciously commit to express ourselves creatively by sharing them with others, we become fulfilled. This purpose gives us the sense of connection and the meaning that we crave in life and that we deserve.

We have all known or heard about people who have worked for decades, and then soon after retirement they end up dying. Or perhaps we know an artist who gets arthritis and can no longer paint and thus does not want to live. When we fail to have, or have and lose, the creative spiritual energy that enables us to experience a connection to our higher self, it can be difficult to see the point in going on.

Purpose is rooted in desire. We may desire a cone of ice cream and be able to get it, thus fulfilling our desire for the moment. However, when a true desire gives itself a method of expression it becomes a purpose. Neither our physical nor emotional body is interested in purpose; purpose is the manifestation of our spiritual body, which bears the essence of our higher self. Realization of purpose is our ultimate fulfillment.

We start our journey here on earth as a toddler, unaware of our full potential and wisdom, beginning to climbing the mountain of life in our own way. As we evolve, the climb becomes easier. We sustain cuts and bruises, and experience fear, joy, and pain along the way. As we reach the mountain top, our aging body is a living record of all of our human experiences, and the wrinkles are the proof. At the top, we finally see what we have not been able to see, able at last to comprehend that our "higher purpose" was to achieve Christ—or Buddha-like consciousness through doing God's work in human form. As our work is done in this body, reconnecting with our highest self becomes our lasting final experience.

Love

> *You don't need to seek love; you need to seek the ways in which you are stopping love from expressing itself.*
> —Rumie

Although the seeds of love were given to you at birth, what germinates true love is the amount of unconditional nurturing and the emotions you experience in early life. Love is a way of connecting to the core of every living thing. How much real love we want to experience has primarily to do with how open we are to experiencing it without judgment.

Imagine all the things you love—your spouse, your children, your hobby, your work—now imagine that your love for all of these things disappeared. What kind of a world would you be living in? Without love there is no happiness; your world would be like living in a big cave in which all you hear is your own echo.

For many, love feels like an emotion that is a separate entity from the self. When we say, "I'm falling in love," we are merely describing the biochemical changes in the body. However, love is a wonderful way of connecting to the core of every living thing.

Imagine you are sitting in a dark room with just a crack of sunlight coming through the door. You experience only a glimmer of light. As you open the door slightly, you see more light and feel more heat. If you decide to open the door wide, you will realize the full strength of the light. So it is with love. Without love there is no truth, no meaning, and no connection. We see this clearly when one member of a couple who has been together for many years and have become soul mates suddenly dies. Often, the surviving spouse loses his will to live. No amount of comfort, emotional support, or money can ease the pain of losing this core connection.

All feelings emanate from love; therefore taking ownership our feelings is the way to self-love. True love comes unconditional acceptance of who we are, both from ourselves and from others. Unlike what most people believe, love is not an emotion. This is one of the reasons why most of us have difficulty differentiating between loneliness and aloneness. Aloneness is a state of being, while loneliness is a state of absence of love. But for many of us, when we feel alone, we react to it by believing that we are lonely. This is evident in dependent or abusive relationships in which the abused person, faced with the possibility of losing the relationship, often chooses to stay in it. Since fear of being alone is perceived as loneliness, the person may stay in an abusive relationship no matter how painful it is. Her subconscious mind considers the perceived choice—the pain of the relationship versus the pain of aloneness. Since the subconscious mind prefers what is familiar, it decides to stay in the relationship.

Love emanates from our spiritual body, which shapes us as a human. Love is probably very frustrating to the field of science since it can't be defined in scientific terms. Therein lies the mystery and art of a higher power. Without love we are zombies. Without love we are lonely. Love is the core of our happiness and the energy that makes our engine work. Since love is ultimately a shared experience, our true happiness comes from those whom we love and those who love us for who we are, unconditionally. As the importance of everything fades as we age, love becomes the most important factor in our lives—the only thing that persists deep within our soul. Love cannot be lost since it is the essence of our being. We are love. It is the ultimate everlasting gift of God or our highest self.

CHAPTER 3   *Emotional Intelligence*

> *It is very important to understand that emotional intelligence is not the opposite of intelligence, it is not the triumph of heart over head—it is the unique intersection of both.*
>
> —David Caruso

Traditionally, intelligence assessments have focused on measuring one's intelligence quotient (IQ) using a variety of standardized tests. More recently, however, the psychological community has become increasingly aware that emotional intelligence has as much importance as IQ, if not more. Emotional intelligence, similar to psychological resilience, has to do with the ability to monitor and process emotions, to have empathy for others, and to handle conflicts in relationships. Emotions are an important source of information and feedback that help direct our behaviors, influence our social interactions, and drive our intuition (gut feelings). To gain a better understanding of your emotional intelligence, take the test that begins on page 137.

For a long time, scientists have argued whether or not our personalities are primarily shaped by genetic components. But how well we come to understand our emotions is shaped primarily by our parents and/or other primary caregivers and the environment in which we were raised.

Environmental factors and emotional interactions in our first few years of life also have a great degree of influence on brain development. Although the brain continues to be shaped throughout our lives, it evolves in complexity at a greater rate during the first few years that at any other time. By the age of three, 9 percent of brain development has already occurred.[21] The human brain evolves in stages, beginning with the visceral brain, followed by the emotional brain, and lastly the intellectual brain. Most of our reality, the way in which we understand the world, is formed during visceral and emotional brain development. Further brain development expands upon this foundation, providing the icing on the cake.

Parents, who understand the importance of developing early emotional intelligence pay attention to their child's nonverbal communication, are able to validate the child's emotions, always encourage their child to express emotions, are not afraid of setting basic limits, and are willing to set a foundation for discipline and social skills. Children are like walking movie cameras; recording their parents' emotional interactions with themselves as well as with each other. Understanding and expressing emotions is primarily a learned and mirroring experience.

Studies clearly show that even an unborn child perceives what kind of a world his mother lives in based on her anxiety level. A mother who is under a great deal of stress during pregnancy produces large amounts of stress hormones (for example, cortisol), which then transfer to the unborn baby, preparing him physiologically for the world into which he will be born. It is a common but significant mistake to assume that unborn or newborn babies are not affected by what is going on around them—not only are they affected at the time, but the impacts of these experiences linger throughout their lifetime.

---

[2] Clinical Endocrinology, May, 2007.

Feelings are not a choice. They are part of the basic need of every human being to connect to and understand his world. Therefore, a child raised in an environment in which he is deprived of experiencing and expressing feelings will suffer greatly. But how does such emotional deprivation occur? Many parents feel very uncomfortable with their feelings due to the environment in which they were raised. This discomfort is easily detected by children, even newborns. The message that is sent through this discomfort is that emotions are not safe. It is this message upon which the child forms his belief about his world and about what he must do within it to survive.

When parents are uncomfortable with certain feelings within themselves they frequently try to repress similar feelings in their children. Children, especially during their first five years, are very perceptive of their environment. They sense their parents' need to hide certain emotions, as a result end up acting those emotions out instead. Parents who experienced an emotionally limited childhood often seek (subconsciously) to live a more emotionally fulfilling life through their children without even realizing it. For example, a parent who was not allowed to get angry growing up, and as an adult feels trapped in monotonous relationship and unfulfilled, may direct his son toward certain sports in which the parent had always wanted to take part, even though his son is not interested. In his mind, the parent takes part in his son's aggression on the field. When children are made to feel that their feelings are not important, they interpret this to mean that the whole of their being is not important, and as a result often don't act in their own best interest. They learn very early on that feelings that can't be expressed must be acted out, even though doing so produces negative consequences.

As children grow up, moving out of a dependency and more toward independence in adolescence, they try to make some sense out of all of these emotions and issues. They try to understand themselves and make some sense of the world amidst a mass of emotional and sexual confusion, but instead they often master the defenses they learned early on for self-preservation.

Healthy, functional human being

Very often I have been asked, "What is a normal family?" Instead of addressing the concept of "normal," my preferred response is that a healthy, functional family is one that equips the children with the intellectual, relationship, and emotional skills they need to deal with life as an adolescent and an adult. A functional family prepares the children to cope with the world. It teaches them how to think clearly and accurately without distortions or denial. It teaches them how to see reality more or less for what it is. A functional family teaches the children how to relate to other human beings in a productive manner while modeling healthy love. It teaches the children how to feel. It teaches them how to recognize feelings, identify them, and express them to other people. It teaches them to care about how others feel and to be able to listen to and respond to those feelings.

Children who come from healthy families have programmed in their subconscious how to relate in a productive, intimate manner with others. Children who come from dysfunctional families have a subconscious programmed by habitually relating to others in a way that destroys intimacy. In my personal estimation, approximately 70 to 80 percent of families are dysfunctional. So perhaps a "normal" family is a dysfunctional family!

As we look back and wonder what kind of emotional guidance we received from our parents, we often come up empty. Many of us who struggle with our emotions have parents who faced the same struggles. Most often, we find that we have either taken the emotional skills we were taught and concluded that what we learned was the absolute truth, or we resent not being taught sufficient emotional skills and vow to be different with our own children.

As children we rely heavily on our parents in order to make sense of our feelings. The feelings that are sent from parent to a child are often mirrored back to the parents. Therefore it is imperative that a child's emotional needs be met. Otherwise, the child will formulate a lifestyle around trying to meet those needs, even though the formula repeatedly fails him.

Children who are raised in an "emotionally open family" witness comfortable, positive emotional interaction between their parents and experience emotional acceptance. These children come to believe that emotions are a healthy and normal part of human interactions. As they grow, they tend to be confident and assertive, and have high self-esteem.

When children grow up in an "emotionally closed family" with negative emotional interactions between their parents, they develop a negative self-image based on the belief that nothing positive can come from an environment that is so negative. Not surprisingly, these children adopt a very negative persona, interpreting their parents' coldness to one another, fighting, or even violence as a standard form of communication. They also learn that these behaviors are how people convey emotions to one another, and since this is unpleasant, they learn to repress their emotions as a way to cope with the world in which they need to survive.

Sometimes, as in families in which domestic violence, rage, and abuse take place, children will learn to not only repress their emotions but actually dissociate themselves from them. This is an extreme means of self-protection, yet sometimes necessary for the child to emotionally survive. In volatile families in which the environment is constantly changing, children may develop different personalities in an attempt to protect themselves from varied physical and/or emotional assaults.

Regardless of the degree to which emotions are suppressed or the specific defenses erected for this purpose, these defenses ultimately work against us, keeping us stuck in survival mode, unable to thrive and grow emotionally. Because of this, it is not uncommon to meet someone who is thirty-five years old but who has the emotional intelligence of a teenager. Perhaps you've been on a date with such a person, at some point asking yourself, "What on earth am I doing here?" or feeling as if you were babysitting a child. Sadly, this happens all the time.

Emotional safety

Why do we like to be hugged? Because it reassures us that we are safe and it comforts us. When someone is crying and we hold them, we are providing emotional safety.

Families that are comfortable with feeling and communicating emotions establish two important building blocks: safety and acceptance. Self-acceptance and self-esteem are established based upon these two factors. Self-esteem is the way in which our parents loved and accepted us. Hence, children who are emotionally accepted by their parents early on and felt emotionally free to be themselves develop higher self-esteem and are naturally more outgoing and confident. As the child learns that it is not wrong to feel as he does, he takes solid steps toward establishing a healthy sense of self-worth. These children tend to admit their mistakes without the need to defend them and understand their humanness. Such people establish belief systems around this understanding, which makes them humble and down-to-earth as they get older. Many people take classes on improving self-esteem, or enroll their children in various activities for the purpose of building self-esteem; self-esteem cannot be "taught."

Safety is a dependency need. We all want to feel safe and protected especially during early childhood. But emotional safety is just as important as physical safety. A child who was provided total physical safety but no emotional safety will not escape the lifelong consequences of such deprivation. When a child expresses emotion, he is taking a risk, exposing a core part of himself. If his parents respond positively to this expression, communicating that it is OK to express the emotion, regardless of what it is, the child feels emotionally safe, self-assured, and becomes well-grounded. As the child grows older he is able to risk easily, trusting that his emotions are on solid ground, and is confident in his decision-making capabilities. The ability to risk and to be open to being vulnerable becomes part of his belief system—a healthy belief system that will serve him well in all aspects of life, including the ability to form intimate relationships. A good metaphor for emotional safety is a bridge. If the bridge is built on a solid foundation (of emotional safety), we can cross the bridge without much concern, but if the foundation is weak, as in a rope bridge, we battle our fear as we make the journey across it.

In early life, when children feel as if their emotions don't matter, they come to believe that something is wrong with them, that they don't matter, and as a result become doubtful and confused. They feel, "I am only lovable when I am not emotionally myself." The mistaken belief of worthlessness is established in our subconscious mind where it haunts us for the rest of our lives. Undoubtedly, a child who experiences a lack of physical safety often has a similar emotional experience as his emotional body is in constant state of fight or flight.

Repressing and/or detaching from our feelings sometimes leads us to believe that other people's feelings are more important than our own, and thus we adopt those feelings as if they are our own. Growing up fearful about upsetting others, and not rocking the boat become more important than our own emotional growth.

Children raised in emotionally anemic families quickly learn that their emotional openness will be met by a reprimand or a manipulative effort to create doubt that their feelings are correct. They are told to shut up, they are told that children are to be seen but not heard, and in some cases if the child expresses his anger to a parent his mouth is washed out with soap. So the message is sent that being emotionally open and expressive is wrong and unsafe. In response, the child begins to tell the parent what he wants to hear rather than what he really feels, to please him and those around him. He doesn't want to disappoint or burden the parent with his emotions and risk losing his parent's love.

When we are raised in emotionally anemic families, we carry this skewed belief system into our adult life, causing us to avoid being vulnerable due to fear of rejection or loss of love. This becomes a problem in romantic relationships. Problems with intimacy and commitment start to surface, but we perceive these issues as normal.

> *A man swayed by negative emotions may have good enough intentions, may be truthful in word, but will never find the truth.*
> —Ghandi

Positive vs. Negative Feelings

> *A clear understanding of negative feelings dismisses them.*
> —Vernon Howard

In many cultures, we learn very early in life to avoid our feelings, especially those we perceive as negative. Our perception is that negative feelings are bad, that nobody wants to hear them anyway, and that they may lead to rejection or punishment. So we hold them in or pretend they don't exist.

As we reach adulthood, not only do our beliefs about how to deal with negative feelings continue, but we learn new defenses to mask them. Our belief is anchored in the mind-set that people won't love and accept us if we have negative feelings.

Jane felt devastated when she found out that her boyfriend decided to go back to his country permanently and ended their relationship. She cried throughout the therapy session and expressed her disappointment and overwhelming sadness. When she left my office, her eyes were swollen and red, her face was pale, and she was clutching a bunch of tissues in her hand, unable to hide her grief. Unfortunately, in the waiting room, she found her friend, who was scheduled to see me. The friend asked

Jane, "How are you?" Jane quickly responded with a smile and said, "I'm fine."

Jane's transformation from a real self to social self was almost instant and subconscious. Fear of rejection resulted in an immediate pretense to preserve her projected ego. For many of us, our self-image must be maintained at all cost. Therefore, we go about our daily lives by telling people we are fine when we are not.

The six basic feelings are happy, sad, angry, afraid, guilt, and hurt. Which of these are negative? Which are positive? The truth is that feelings are neither positive nor negative. They are what they are. What leads to the perception of them as positive or negative is the way in which we come to terms with them.

The feeling of anger is often perceived as negative, and for that very reason some people are afraid of getting angry or showing it.

Let's say you are preparing for a big family gathering. While you are busy cooking, you glance out into the backyard and notice your son's uncle touching your son inappropriately. What would be your first feeling? What would you do? Most likely the feeling you would experience is anger, and you would immediately intervene and protect your child. Because of the anger you felt, you were able to act accordingly to bring about a positive outcome. But imagine for a moment the outcome if this event did not make you feel angry, or that you felt fear and guilt instead and you doubted the validity of your primary feeling. What if fear of rocking the boat, or unwillingness to upset the uncle, or fear of how the uncle may feel if you confronted this situation became your primary concern? Unable to identify or respond to your anger in a timely manner at that moment would turn anger for you into a negative emotion.

CHAPTER 4   *Emotional Self Mastery*

> *Often the hands will solve a mystery that the intellect has struggled in vain.*
> —Carl Jung

Emotional mastery is a work of art. By understanding the scientific and psychological aspects of this natural process, you are on your way to discovering the secrets of emotional wealth. But for some of you, the journey will be an uphill battle to the end if you are unable to recognize that you are a work of your own art.

We all want a stress-free mind and body, and many of us seek to enhance our personal development to improve our quality of life. However, feeling rundown, stressed, emotionally overwhelmed, and yet still continuing on the same path hoping that it will change becomes a way of life. You may be emotionally bankrupt and not even know it. For some of us, feeling overwhelmed or stressed feels normal because of how we perceive the world. Some of us formed a belief that the only way we matter is by giving to others, even though there is not much of anything left to take care of our own emotional needs. Some of us arrived at a belief that the world owes us and can't seem to receive enough, always wanting more. No matter how much others take, we are unable to satiate our emotional hunger and still feel empty. We are constantly plagued by this nagging void, trying desperately to hide it. We believe in the illusion of a missing piece that will bring us ultimate happiness and search relentlessly to find it. As we reach out in our desperation for some sense of emotional fulfillment, we may be setting ourselves up for disappointments without realizing it. This relentless pursuit of emotional fulfillment and happiness outside ourselves creates misguided beliefs that cause us to search for answers outside our own bodies. But sustainable emotional self mastery and a healthier lifestyle are possible.

When we are grounded in honesty around our core feelings, we are ultimately rewarded with everlasting emotional self mastery that cannot be lost. Such a state influences our behavior and thoughts in very positive ways. Those of us who are emotionally wealthy need nothing. We are no longer in search of happiness because we are one with ourselves. We have relinquished our need for quick fixes because we are grounded in the pleasure of self-contentment.

Mary had been in therapy for twelve years dealing with her childhood molestation issues. She had also attended three different workshops on trauma resolution. She said that she always felt good during the therapeutic process, and did a lot of crying, however, the painful feelings always came back. As she told me about her experiences, she began to cry. I interrupted her and asked how she was feeling. She said she felt devastated. I pressed by asking again how she was feeling. She said she felt awful. I asked her if she could identify how she felt using the core feelings: angry, sad, happy, hurt, afraid, and ashamed. She said she felt confused.

It is important to identify with the six core feelings. Because they are simple and easily identifiable, and focusing on them stops us from going "into our head" to try to figure out their meaning. This enables us to focus on our heart and chest area where we mostly experience feelings—hence the term "gut feeling."

Mary was clearly having difficulty identifying her feelings. As a result, her responses were more likely what she thought she should be feeling. When we cannot identify with our true core feelings, we often create what I call secondary reactive feelings, which give us the illusion of being in touch with our feelings. Some examples of secondary reactive feelings are self-pity, frustration, persistent guilt, indifference, and confusion. When we use these words we may believe we are in touch with our feelings, but in reality we become further alienated from our core feelings. When we fear expressing our true feelings, we often act in a way that helps others experience what we are feeling. For example, while we may be unable to identify that we are sad, we cry to communicate how we are feeling.

Failure to identify with feelings distorts our reality and affects our perceptions. The more we distance ourselves from our feelings, the more we become emotionally anemic. Achieving emotional self mastery is a unique process of connecting to our feelings, following a commonsense approach that brings about the changes we desire.

The process of achieving emotional self mastery contains four primary components:

- Learning how to identify core feelings
- Understanding of six core feelings
- Learning how to process feelings
- Re-programming mistaken beliefs

Feelings vs. Emotions

> *Having emotions is one thing, but knowing them is a different matter.*
> —Casey

It is a common misperception that "feelings" and "emotions" are the same thing. Not true. Feelings tend to be immediate, based on the moment, and easily identifiable. For example, when we stop to smell a rose, we experience an immediate feeling without any thought. However, emotions tend to be an accumulation of many different thoughts and feelings over time. In other words, our feelings are like raindrops, which accumulate to create the pond that is our emotions.

Feelings exist more on the surface, while emotions tend to run deeper. For this reason, when an event occurs, we access our feelings before we access our emotions. For instance, when a mother loses her child in a department store and then finds him hiding inside a rack of clothes, she feels angry and yells at him. But her core emotion is likely fear.

Failure to identify and process core feelings has a cumulative effect; leaving many of us emotionally overwhelmed. For this reason, many of us struggle when attempting to resolve emotional conflicts or may not experience any sense of real healing in therapy. What is necessary to truly resolve issues is the journey toward emotional self mastery, which starts with mastering our core feelings.

We all have feelings and some of us feel more than others. But feeling alone seldom leads to emotional mastery. Many of us struggle when attempting to get in touch with our feelings because it does not seem natural for us. So we over identify with certain feelings with which we are most comfortable, such as anger, guilt, or fear, even though that may not be the actual core feeling we are experiencing.

Some of us respond to feelings with our brain—we think to feel. In other words, when asked how we feel, we respond by rolling our eyes toward the top of our head, searching for an intellectual answer, and then responding with what we think we must be feeling. Without even realizing it, we are simply attempting to explain the feeling at the moment rather than expressing it. Most of the time those of us who think to feel vacillate between happy and angry throughout the day.

We discussed previously the importance of the mind-body connection. Because of this powerful connection, when we distance ourselves from our core feelings we also attempt to repress or dissociate from our emotional body. But this violates our basic nature. While we create the illusion that our feelings are under control, our physical body continues to feel those emotions as discomfort or stress in some part of our body. As our need to avoid emotions gradually increases, so does the need to process emotions in our head by relying heavily on brain processing power in order to make some sense of our world. Intellect and reasoning are important. However, when they become disconnected from feelings, they lead us to inhuman and self-destructive lifestyles. This is evident in people who have addiction disorders. The more distant we are from our feelings, the more distant we become from our human qualities. No wonder people's lives become more complicated over a period of time as they continue to use ineffective tools to deal with their feelings!

Identifying True Feelings

We alone are responsible for our own feelings. But what good are feelings if we cannot identify with them? No wonder Star Trek's Mr. Spock envied the humans' ability to feel and connect, as he was only capable of logic.

Again, the six core feelings are anger, sad, happy, afraid, ashamed, and hurt. Here is a quick test: Close your eyes and clear your head for a few seconds and then try to repeat what the six core feelings are. Make a note of which feelings you remembered easily and which you could not or struggled to recall. For many of us, it's not as easy as it sounds.

We have all memorized a wide variety of information in our lives—why is it that remembering these six simple words is often a struggle? It is probably not because we are having a sudden memory lapse or were not paying attention. More likely, one of two things occurred. Either 1) our subconscious defenses were employed immediately to maintain the status quo, thereby reinforcing it and creating a sense of comfort, or 2) we can't remember some of the feelings because those feelings are the ones troubling us the most and/or are the ones that we are running away from. One of my clients, a successful surgeon, said, "I can read a whole book and summarize it for you with ease, but remembering these six feelings is like trying to remember all the books in a library."

This simple yet powerful diagnostic tool provides many answers as to what went wrong emotionally in our early lives and what emotions we decided to block or avoid as a result of it. The more we defend those emotions, the more we come to identify with our defenses and rely on them as the truth to make sense of our world. This is one of the reasons why we may resist and become reactive if anything challenges those defenses. Hence, when we start doing the feelings check, we initially run into the defenses we have erected to hide those painful emotions.

Feelings Check

Every day we go about our business without paying much attention to our feelings unless something happens that causes us to feel (e.g., another driver cuts us off and we feel anger, or another driver slows down to allow us to merge in front of him and we feel grateful). When we take our feelings for granted, we live a knee-jerk, reactionary lifestyle. But when we consciously start paying attention to our feelings in the present we become grounded and remain connected to our inner selves.

One of the best ways to get "out of our head" and start connecting with our feelings is by doing a feelings check. Simply ask yourself, "How am I feeling right now?" and try to identify with any of the six core feelings. It is best to concentrate around your heart region and see what it feels like. Initially you may find yourself struggling to identify with your feeling due to your subconscious conditioning. That's OK. This can take time. But by simply becoming aware that you are disconnected from your core feelings you are taking the first step on your journey toward emotional self mastery.

Practice

To help create awareness of your core emotions, you may want to establish visual reminders such as writing the six core emotions on the mirror, or on a piece of paper that sits on top of your desk. These visual aids enable you to check in with this list on a regular basis so that you gradually establish a sense of comfort with your feelings. As you achieve this mind-set, the need to go into your head for answers will diminish.

One day while I was at a toy store with my daughter, I saw a miniature Snow White and the Seven Dwarfs. I purchased them, gave the Snow White to my daughter, and renamed the dwarfs Happy, Sad, Angry, Scared, Ashamed, Hurt (the seventh dwarf represents emotional dwarfism!). They still sit on my desk, a constant reminder of the six core emotions, as well as a great conversation piece. As I befriended my emotions, I have achieved greater emotional clarity, and my work has become more rewarding. I cannot overemphasize the importance of learning to identify our true feelings.

Let's assume you took your six kids to a playground where there were many other kids playing. But when it was time to go, you could not identify your own kids! You could not remember their names! Would you take home someone else's kids, pretend as if they are your own, and rename them? Would you abandon your kids simply because it's too much work to find them? Would you pretend they didn't exist and just walk away? Of course the answer to all of the previous questions is "no." If we did any of these things, what kind of a parent would we be? "Insane" we may say. Or "abusive." Yet many of us treat our feelings equal disregard, denial, and avoidance. And we wonder why so many of us are not emotionally grounded.

We are our feelings—we cannot separate the two. The more we try to deny them, the more distorted we become. We end up living the lies we create, relying on denial as our savior, until we ultimately start believing the lies are reality.

Jill, who has been married for seven years, watched her husband flirt with other women on a regular basis. Even though her feelings of hurt, anger, and shame were constant reminders of her failing relationships, she gradually mastered the art of pretense, giving others the impression that she was not bothered by her husband's behaviors. When some of her friends told her that her husband had hit on them, she just laughed and remarked, "That's just the way Mike is, he has always been that way." After a while, she experienced doubt, confusion, and could no longer trust her eyes and ears. One day, she found her husband in bed with her best friend. She blamed herself. As Jill disregarded her true feelings by pretending they did not matter, her life became as pretentious as her distorted perception, and her pretense ultimately became her reality.

When we betray ourselves emotionally, we cheat ourselves from living a fulfilling life. We blame others for who we are, where we are, and what has happened to us. To achieve emotional wealth, we must abandon this learned powerlessness, this helplessness, this victim mentality. We must take the initiative to change the world within us, to learn to check in with and identify our core feelings, and to do the necessary work for a successfully journey toward emotional self mastery.

CHAPTER 5

Feelings

> *Understanding a problem is only the gateway to the feelings, the feelings are where the problem is solved.*
> —Casey

We are energy and so are our feelings. In physics, for instance, we can explain why when we drop a beach ball into a pool it floats. Similarly, we can use this action as a metaphor to understand feelings. Imagine you are standing in the middle of a pool of water, which represents you, holding a beach ball, which represents anger. When you drop the beach ball, it naturally floats away on the surface of the water, much like feelings drift along the current of your creative energy. But what if you don't want anyone to see this beach ball of anger, and push it underwater to hide it? Of course, this takes a lot of energy as the ball naturally resists such force, struggling to come to the surface. Similarly, it takes a lot of energy to repress our feelings; it is an unnatural process that depletes our energy. The deeper we try to push the beach ball down, the more intensely it will fight to return to the surface, often shooting up out of the water. In much the same way, as we push anger deeper and deeper, we become more reactive and may explode in a rage. Now imagine you decide to try to keep fifteen beach balls under water! How about one hundred? Imagine the amount of energy and effort it would take to manage such an ordeal! Now add to the mix, while managing all those beach balls, taking care of the kids, going to work, running errands, etc.! This clearly describes a life of exhaustion and chaos. Yet this juggling act is not only perceived as normal but often admired as talented multitasking. Day after day, year after year, relentlessly reinforcing this emotional escapism gradually depletes our emotional energy, leaving us feeling run down and depressed. The more energy we devote to altering the natural direction of our feelings, the more we alter the direction of our lives in negative ways. As we fight our basic nature, we become our own worst enemy.

You may be asking yourself at this point, "Why do I get in the way of my own feelings? Is there another way to be?" If you believe you deserve more, then you must commit to do the healing work. Your life can either be fulfilling or empty—the amount of work is the same.

One day while I was sitting in a dental office, I noticed a beautiful aquarium sitting in the corner of the waiting room. I could not help admiring how the air bubbles floated gently from the bottom of the tank to the surface and then burst open, naturally and effortlessly releasing their energy. Suddenly, it occurred to me that the body of water was representative of our physical body, the air bubbles modeling the emotions that are created within it. I tried to change this process, by putting a cup over the air bubbles to stop them from reaching the surface. For a brief moment it appeared that I had achieved the goal, and my intellect concurred with that conclusion. But it soon became evident that those tiny bubbles were joining together and forming larger bubbles, which surfaced much faster and with much greater force. I realized that I had not been able to change this natural process but simply postponed the inevitable.

In much the same way, we try to block our feelings by various means such as drugs and alcohol, intellectualization, justification, avoidance, etc. While these defenses may work for a short time, they cannot postpone the inevitable. So if we know that these measures do not work for us, why do we continue to repeat them? As the saying goes, the definition of insanity is doing the same thing over and over again but expecting different results. The reason we do this is because our established belief system tells us that we must avoid our feelings at all cost even if our prior attempts to do so have failed miserably. This is why alcoholics drink to escape pain and then, despite waking up the next morning in even more pain, soon drink again.

We all feel experience feelings deep within us, and we need to allow them to come to the surface for release. This is the way were created; the longer we continue to fight our basic nature, the longer we will continue to struggle.

Starting early in life, we were taught to think and memorize, and as we go through life, we'd rather talk about issues, thoughts, and events. So the acceptable form of communication is therefore based around what we think and not what we feel. Do you remember any kind of guidance from your parents about how to identify or express your feelings? Likely not. In our early years, many of us may not even have heard the names of the six core feelings.

People who live in a state of confusion, frustration, and anxiety likely don't know the meaning of the six core feelings. Defining our feelings is imperative if we want to get to the root of our emotional issues. When we see red, yellow, and green colored circles on a piece of paper, our mind perceives them simply as colored circles. We don't have much reaction. But when we see traffic lights—the same colors—our reaction is very different as these colors now have a different meaning. When we don't learn the true definition of the six core feelings, we end up giving our own definition and meaning to each feeling based upon our beliefs and what we've learned from others. Defining and understanding each and every core feeling keeps us not only grounded but also directs us toward a proper response.

Imagine throwing darts at a dart board blindfolded. You may eventually hit the bull's-eye after many unsuccessful attempts, but you'll likely be so frustrated and exhausted by that time that you won't even enjoy the achievement.

> *When something becomes a chore, it's not worth having.*
> —Casey

Defining Feelings

Knowing the definition of each core feeling is like being in a dark room with a flashlight, knowing how you can find your way out with ease. This natural process is empowering as well as enlightening, providing the gateway for higher consciousness. The alternative is to continue in the dark, making it a chore, bumping your head, and struggling to find a way out. Ultimately you may find the door after an exhausting, painful experience, but the outcome becomes one of chaos, including self-rejection and loss of self.

> *You cannot deal with what you don't know, and what you don't know may deal you a lifetime of misery.*
> —Casey

See if you can answer the following questions—write down your answers for later comparison.

- What is the definition of fear?
- What is the definition of guilt?

Happy

You come to work feeling wonderful. When your coworker asks, "How are you this morning?" you answer, "I'm happy."

Happy is knowing what you want and having what you want. It is a state of balance, a sense of well-being. It is knowing that nothing bad is happening to you at this time in your life. It is a state of contentment. Your body is saturated with positive, creative energy.

Fear

Later that day, you learn that your best friend was in a car accident and that he's in the hospital in the intensive care unit. How do you feel?

Fear is when your body alerts you that you are in imminent danger of getting hurt or losing someone or something important to you.

In humans, as in animals, survival is instinctual. It's the emotion of fear that makes us react to an imminent threat and seek safety. In the case of this example, while it's not your own life that is threatened, your friend's life is in jeopardy. The threat that you are about to lose a loved one, at this moment, is a real fear.

Less dramatically, you may be facing serious financial problems, such as your home being in foreclosure. The threat of losing your home is a real fear.

Sad

A few hours later your friend remains in the intensive care unit. Although an element of fear lingers, sadness envelops you.

Feeling sad comes from sudden disappointment or is a leftover residue from pain. Feeling sad often triggers tears, which allows us to release the feelings. The grieving process is only possible if we are in touch with our feelings of sadness.

Hurt

The next day you learn that your friend died during the night. Your sadness is largely replaced by an overwhelming hurt.

Hurt is about the loss of a loved one or the loss of oneself. The transformation of emotional energy from sadness to hurt is immediate, obvious, and almost paralyzing. While most hurt carries some element of sadness, the two emotions have different vibrational energy. Because we experience hurt energy differently, our response is also different. Engulfed in the painful energy, we may be unable stop crying, unable to sleep, and unable to eat.

For many of us, hurt is a very difficult feeling to face. How we deal with it determines our emotional future.

Anger

You do not want to talk about the loss of your friend. You stuff your emotion deep down; you bottle it up. You become irritable, short-tempered, and more and more reactive to people around you. And you don't know why.

Most anger is hurt that is aging. Like old garbage, the longer you hold it, the worse it smells. The hurt we repress changes its energy and resurfaces in the form of anger. Although there may be some minor events that may cause us to feel some anger, when we overreact, it is a clear indication that our anger is about more than the triggering event. We may try to justify such anger by blaming others or circumstances, trying to evade the truth. The result is that we avoid the real hurt and the anger that it bears, ultimately suffering long-term consequences.

Guilt

You continue to avoid your hurt and anger. As the energy of these emotions slowly transforms to a different vibrational level, you experience guilt. You start to doubt yourself, feel responsible for what happened, regret that you failed to go to the hospital. Through this guilt, you can continue to bypass your hurt and anger, wallowing in self-pity.

Guilt is anger turned against the self. People who are brought up uncomfortable with getting angry or unable to express anger tend to adopt guilt as a way of responding to the world. Guilt is the ultimate declaration of helplessness.

Depression

Just a few days ago, life was good. You were happy. Then you lost your dear friend, which ultimately brought you to the point of depression.

Depression is not an emotion. Although no single cause of depression has been identified, it appears that interaction among genetic, biochemical, environmental, and psychosocial factors may play a role. However, nonclinical depression is simply the accumulation of negative emotions that overwhelm us to the point of being paralyzed. As more guilt and pain are repressed, it becomes more and more difficult to experience joy or happiness. We gradually start losing interest in things that used to be important.

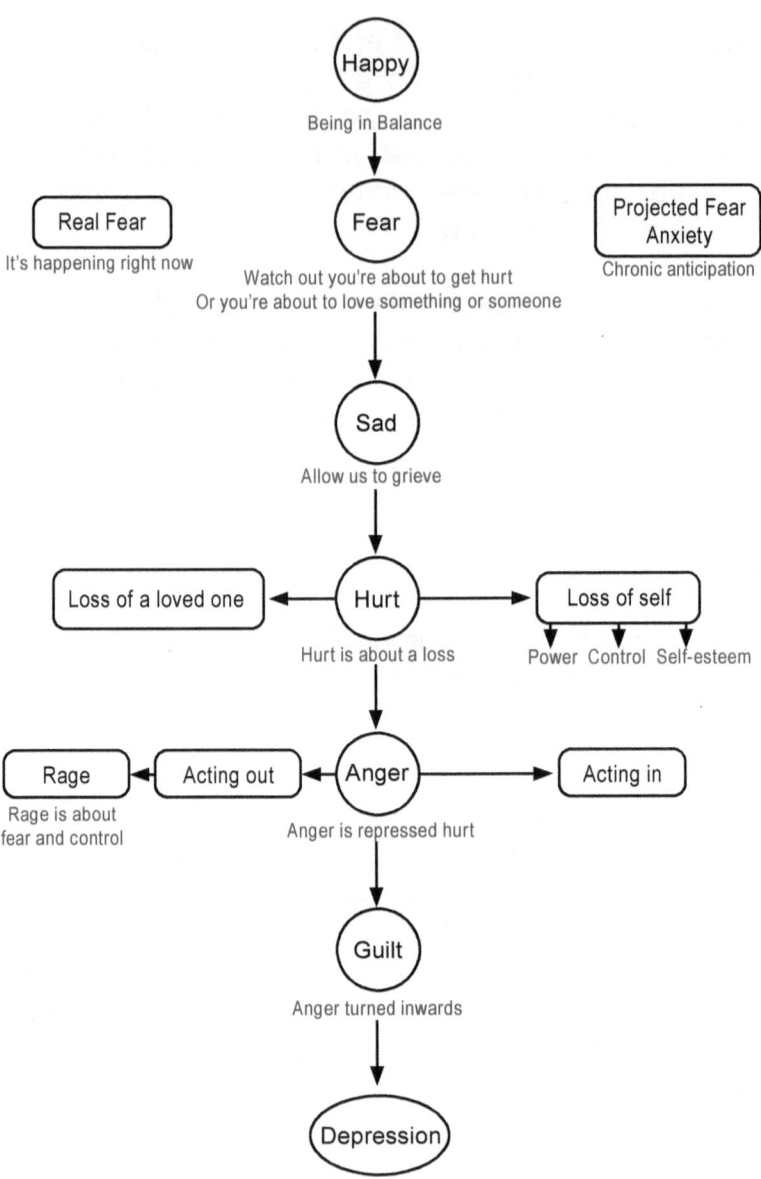

It is important to note, however, that clinical depression is different. Although anyone can develop depression, some types of depression, including major depression, seem to run in families. Whether or not depression is genetic, the disorder is believed to be associated with changes in levels of chemical in the brain such as serotonin and norephinephrine.

Sometimes a single event can turn our lives upside down, while other times the cumulative effect of many events and the emotions associated with them take us down an unhealthy path. Unfortunately many of us suffer throughout our lives even as our emotional issues are evident to others. Holding on to a false façade simply prolongs our suffering. Until we surrender to the ultimate truth about who we really are and learn to master our emotions, we will continue to deceive ourselves, living the lies we fabricate as truth.

We each have the choice to be happy or depressed, but the amount of work is the same.

CHAPTER 6

Understanding Core Feelings

> *The ultimate value of life depends upon awareness and the power of contemplation rather than upon mere survival.*
>
> —Casey

We are each unique beings, experiencing our own feelings, and as a result, creators of our own world. As we better understand and accept our feelings, our need to defend and repress them becomes less important. So it is crucial to know that we either nurture our emotions and enrich ourselves and grow, or invest in our defenses, and as they blur our perception, allow our defensive patterns to gradually become our reality. Our feelings are in constant communication with us. However, lack of proper understanding of these feelings, how they work and what they mean, impacts our lives in negative ways. Whether we realize it or not, we are always feeling, and our feelings change constantly throughout the day. Being in touch with our feelings as they occur provides clarity and a sense of connection to ourselves—we emit the truth of who we really are. I'm sure you have been around someone from whom you could not wait to get away, even though you didn't know much about them. Negative energy radiates and is often very difficult to camouflage.

Happy

> *Fulfillment and contentment are pathways to happiness.*
> —Aristotle

Happy is a feeling of well-being at this moment. We all seem to be striving for happiness, and for some, happiness is the ultimate goal. But you may be surprised to find that happy can be a very negative emotion for some people. This is clearly evident in some people who yearn to be happy, and yet their behaviors and lifestyles reflect the opposite. As previously stated, we define our feelings based upon how we come to terms with them as well as the kind of beliefs we establish early on.

Joe, who has been a recovering addict for many years, in and out of rehab, said, "My life was a roller coaster when I was drinking and after years of therapy I understood why that was. But in sobriety I found myself going through the same roller coaster experience. My life has been about chaos and conflict due to my drinking, and to me that felt normal. When I am sober, the chaos stops; I begin to feel a sense of normalcy, and good things start to come my way. I start feeling happy for the first time. But before you know it, I relapse!"

Joe understood his recovery but did not understand the emotional connection to his relapse. When Joe started feeling happy, subconsciously he started experiencing uneasiness because happy was not one of the feelings he felt comfortable with. This level of uneasiness pushed him into sabotaging his recovery by relapsing so that he could start feeling the familiar chaos, worthlessness, anger, and shame all over again. This is a very common occurrence among recovering addicts. During the first six months of recovery they often relapse, triggered by not being able to manage their anger, and during the next six months, they often relapse because of discomfort with feelings of self-worth and happiness.

Roadblocks to Happiness

When we don't realize we have the power to be happy and learn to exercise that power, we develop a negative behavior pattern, which is very easy to reinforce. It is easy to have a bad time, it's easy to find fault in things—it's also very boring, but it's easy. Unhappy people tend to be very negative, always looking for something wrong with everything to further justify their unhappiness.

For most of us, however, happiness is a state of mind we try to achieve. Of course, the ultimate happiness lies in achieving higher levels of consciousness in which we relinquish our materialistic needs, stripped of our defenses, having dissolved our ego. Happiness is not having what we want but wanting what we have. As stated previously, when we live on a physical plane we become more ego-based, and often define ourselves with materialistic things. Since the ego is insatiable, we are never satisfied. We truly believe that there is something out there that, if we could just attain it, then we will be happy. If we attain it, we experience a short-them fix, an ego boost, but never true joy, satisfaction, peace, or fulfillment. And yet, it doesn't stop us from continuing the vicious cycle. To be happy, we must look for more positive and purposeful things to embrace. Feeling happy is a matter of working on it.

Poor Self-image

We are our own worst critic. Instead of accepting ourselves as a whole, we constantly criticize ourselves. Constant thoughts such as, "I have skinny legs," or "My nose is too big," or "I hate my hair," are strong messages sent routinely to our emotional body where the emotion of anger is attached. Ongoing self-criticism hinders happiness. Total self-acceptance comes from accepting ourselves unconditionally and making the most of what we have rather than wishing for what we would have liked to have. With the invention of plastic surgery, many people are finding themselves undergoing surgeries with the belief that they will attain a perfect, happy self. If the one seeking surgery feels good about herself and simply seeks self-betterment, the surgery will likely be a positive experience. Yet after multiple surgeries, some still can't seem to find the happiness or the perfect self they seek. Instead of searching in mirrors for outer perfection, we must look deep within ourselves to see and accept our imperfections. Only then can we experience happiness.

Being In the Present

Due to past fears and resulting control issues, we may struggle to remain emotionally in the present because it creates a conflict with our personality. Past fears conditioned us to be always on the lookout for any possible injury or threat. Hence we believe, "I will be happy when . . .," a futuristic thinking that hinders our happiness. When we don't understand our feelings, we have no choice but to live in tomorrow land. Many books are written about this subject. People who read them often agree but are unable to practice living in the present. While we may logically understand the power of this information and would like to apply to our lives, our subconscious tends to be habitual by nature; it maintains the status quo. Because we are conditioned to avoid the present, after a while it becomes an automatic response—it is part of our belief system. We must work to reprogram ourselves so that we can be present in ourselves and our emotions at this moment. Remember, tomorrow is promised to no one. Life is happening at this moment. But we need to be in the present to enjoy it.

Discontentment

We all have many desires, which change radically throughout our lives. Failure to pursue our dreams and desires leads to unhappiness. Some of us hope or wish that our desires are going to magically become reality or that someone else is going to make it happen for us. This is a recipe for disappointing life. We need look at ourselves and stop denying the truth. Are we content with our life the way it is? Are we in a romantic relationship with the right person? Are we happy with our job? Are we lost spiritually?

Of course there are many more questions we can ask. But deep down, we already know the truth. The main reason we are not happy is because we are living a life that is the opposite of what we wanted. As a result, whatever we do, whomever we are with, we do not experience contentment and joy. We're like a child who makes a Christmas wish list, but what he gets in return disappoints him. We know what we have been yearning for deep inside, yet we are not allowing ourselves to experience it. We may know this intellectually, but deep within us we believe that we are not deserving. No amount of encouraging words or material support from others will matter unless we learn to feel deserving inside. Only then can we experience true happiness within us and abandon the superficial quest for happiness on the outside.

Toxic Emotions

When we bargain with our feelings by turning them into negative energy, our life becomes a mirror reflection of those trapped emotions. These emotions make us think we are bad. If we trap our pain inside, happiness becomes merely a wish. Toxic emotions rob us of our creative energy and create an unsettled existence. When we suffer emotionally because we have not faced our toxic past, our idea of happiness will manifest itself through instant gratification. We become impulsive. When we feel bored, we may find ourselves shopping, buying things that we don't even need. We may turn to a bottle for relief from our sadness. We may meet someone and want to instantly become sexual. Although these instant gratifications temporarily make us think we are happy, this misguided belief only leads to more self-hatred. We may tell ourselves that we really want to be happy, yet continue to invite unhappiness into our lives. If we don't address this emotional baggage, it will continue to block our happiness.

Fear

> *It is not the fear of the unknown that torments us, it is the fear of the known.*
>
> —Casey

Fear alerts us to an imminent danger so that we can defend ourselves. When a threat lurks, our body responds by producing specific hormones that prepare our muscles for either a fight or flight response. Our physical body responds to our emotional body's signal by reducing the blood flow to certain parts of our body, such as the digestive system, while supplying more blood to our extremities, heart, brain. The mind and body is at work in harmony with no conscious thought.

Real fear is about losing someone or something important and is taking place at this moment. In contrast, false fear or anxiety is about something that is not taking place at this moment. When we are touch with real fear, we are able to respond appropriately to guide ourselves to safety. We are seldom paralyzed with real fear. The ability to face our real fears gives us insight, makes us aware of our limitations, and keeps us honest. This is the primary reason why some of us are able to take regular, healthy risks. Risk-taking and healthy fear are interconnected. The real fear becomes a catalyst for personal growth and finding out our capabilities rather than a hindrance.

We have all had scary dreams in which we find ourselves running from something or someone, or our feet are glued to the ground and we just can't seem to get away. We have no idea what is chasing us, but one thing is clear—we want the dream to be over! Unfortunately for some, such dreams are never-ending. False fear or anxiety results in confusion and further internal chaos. Those consumed with false fear continually ponder, worry, analyze potential outcomes, and become paralyzed with indecisiveness.

As life begins to resemble childhood dreams, day-to-day reinforcement of false fear leads to a life of nightmares.

For many of us, fear is a very difficult feeling to understand and work through. The primary reason for this has a lot do with our inability to separate real fear from anxiety. Many of us suffer from anxiety disorders and can only face the world with antianxiety medications. Ninety percent of anxiety is false fear while the other ten percent is real based on how much fear we experienced early in life and how we came to terms with it.

Unless we understand the difference between real fear and false fear, our happiness will be forever tainted. Over time we have programmed our own mind, thus we must do the hard work of reprogramming it ourselves. We cannot expect miracles—it took years to establish our current belief system. And we cannot blame others for where we are today. But unless we come to terms with fear, we will be haunted by it for the duration of our time on this earth. Following examples of fears are based upon false assumptions or beliefs.

Fear of Failure

Some of us chronically worry and are anxious on a subconscious level. We tend to doubt ourselves, we don't feel worthy; we believe that whatever we do will not be accepted by others, so why bother. We fear not being good enough, not making a mistake or being criticized by others. Hence, a false sense of safety is a trade-off for being happy. The possibility of failure simply doesn't merit the risk of change. By taking no action, our comfort zone is protected, and any chance of positive change is blocked. In this case, the brain acts as the protector of our inner core beliefs, and sabotaging becomes the only way to defend them. Although our comfort zone may not be pleasant, we can survive there.

Fear of Success

Success is something that makes us feel happy. However, if we are not accustomed to feeling happy, projected fear is a convenient way of postponing it. Fear of success is the flip side of fear of failure. Many of us are ultimately scared of unleashing our potential not because we fear we are going to fail, but because we fear our own ability to succeed. We fear moving forward. The idea of embracing happiness and truly succeeding tends to stir up many old self-limiting beliefs that we are not worthy or deserving. So we accept our current fate. Others of us only see the negative reaction we may get from their family or friends if we are successful. We may be concerned about losing the love and acceptance from those around us because those people may become jealous or envious or resent our success. Sometimes our need for stern approval tends to cause us to sabotage our happiness simply because it is not worth the risk of jeopardizing the small amounts of acceptance we currently have. These strong beliefs reveal deep-rooted feelings of self-doubt, which manifest as subconscious self-sabotage. Holding ourselves and our brilliance back truly serves nobody. This is a form of self-abuse.

Projected Anxiety

As we've discussed, anxiety has nothing to do with real fear. Real fear has to do with the present; projected anxiety has to do with future. An anxious person continually anticipates that something bad is going to happen and constantly prepares for the worst.

For example, even though we have been flying for years or taken elevators on many occasions, suddenly some of us find ourselves having uneasy feelings. We may start refusing to get on airplanes or elevators because we feel as if we are about to suffocate, sometimes even gasping for air. We know that airplanes seldom crash, and the possibility of losing our lives is always present, but suddenly these thoughts that did not previously hinder our lives are problematic as we subconsciously drift into a state of anxiety. Preoccupied, constantly anticipating news of the next airplane crash, we justify our unfounded "fear" by inaction. If we look for evidence of anything long enough or hard enough, we will find it. Without realizing it, the moment we find the evidence, our belief reinforces the projected fear as real fear, and we become righteous.

Why do so many of us choose to live our lives in this torturous fashion? The primary purpose of projected anxiety is to avoid our core feelings in the present. In other words, anxiety is a form of defense, enabling us to avoid and distort our reality. When we are in a constant state of "what if," anticipating that something bad will happen, we are not in touch with our feelings. Instead, we are primarily concerned with trying to control the outcome of each situation and minimizing the impact of the injury. This mind-set allows us to check out emotionally and become numb, while at the same time believing that what we are feeling is real fear. Those of us who suffer from anxiety tend to be very controlling by nature. No wonder! We are busy making sure things will go as planned and that the details are well taken care of. We become numb, and the anxiety level climbs. Although control is mostly an illusion, the more we feel out of control emotionally, the more controlling we become. In many cases, the problem with projected anxiety starts in early life due to early childhood experiences, especially if there was an ongoing physical, emotional, or sexual abuse, or abandonment.

Alice talked about what it was like for her between the ages of five and eight. She talked about how some nights her dad would come home from the night club, intoxicated, walk up the wooden stairs, and try to fondle her body before he went to bed. She said it was so frequent an event that the minute she heard the footsteps she would roll onto her stomach and pretend she was asleep. Till this day, every time she hears footsteps she feels like running and hiding under her bed.

Sometimes a certain smell, sight or sound that we associate with a fearful experience will trigger physiological responses. These contextual emotions may even be generalized as we become an adult. Let's say we were punished as a child by being locked up in small room. The fear we felt was difficult to bear, and we cried and screamed to get out. Later in life we may find ourselves having an anxiety attack in an airplane even though we have been flying for years. The ability of such fearful episodes to cause physiological responses years later is largely related to the intensity of the fearful experience and the length of time associated with it.

This phenomenon is obvious in many soldiers who have returned from the battlefields, disabled and unable to have a normal emotional life due to the fear of dying trapped deep within them. Although they know logically that they are now safe, they are unable to control the repressed fear of the battlefield experiences, which keeps surfacing in the form of anxiety and panic attacks. For example, a soldier may hear the sound of a helicopter and run for cover no matter where he is. Many soldiers are diagnosed with post-traumatic stress disorder (PTSD). Although the trapped fears surface, the inability to properly release them causes the soldier to recycle them through nightmares and panic attacks.

When we are subjected to such torturous experiences, the fear of each experience becomes ingrained in our body, our subconscious, and our soul. Those of us who experience repeated fearful experiences cannot escape serious emotional consequences and may end up becoming what I call "fear-based" people. Emotional survival becomes of utmost importance. We are always on guard, anticipating any possible emotional injury. We create a state of anxiety for self-preservation, not realizing that the very thing upon which we rely is also a weapon of self-torture.

Self-conditioning

When we are confronted with imminent fear, for example, if someone is about to assault us, we respond with rapid and shallow breathing, increased heart rate, sweating, shaking, and so on, without intellectual analysis of the situation. This physiological response to possible fear is primarily due to releasing hormones, such as Adrenaline and cortisol, which are responsible for fight-or-flight decisions. So how do we explain suddenly experiencing some or all of these physiological responses while sitting safely in our own home? People around us don't understand what just happened; we feel embarrassed and can't seem to find the words to explain.

There are many similarities between an asthma attack and an anxiety attack. Most asthma attacks are emotionally, not medically, based.[31] Asthma, like anxiety, can be triggered by various trapped emotions (stress, negative emotions, panic) that are seeking an expression resulting in a physical response that torments the body. Anxiety is not any different. Projected anxiety is a self-induced chemical reaction that is primarily the result of a repetitive thought process. When we think something bad is going to happen, our body responds by releasing the cortisol hormone; thus, we feel and react to that emotion. We start believing something bad really is going to happen.

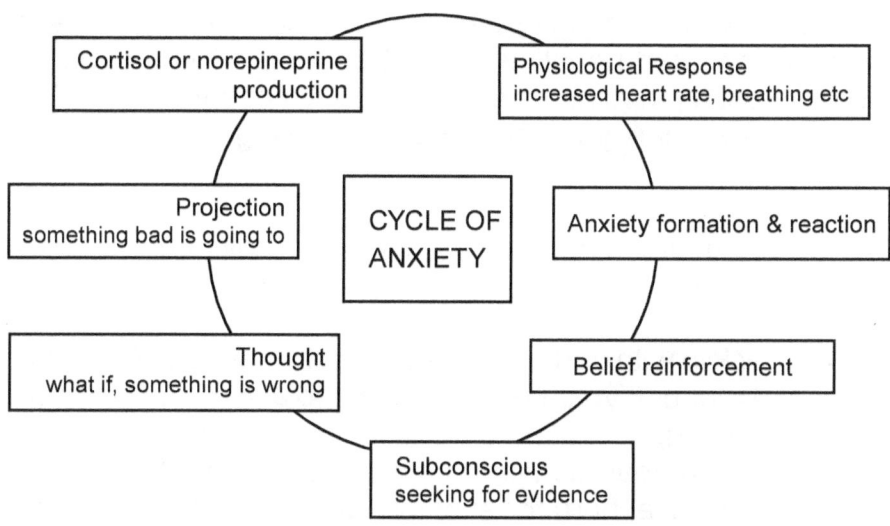

Years of self-conditioning to worry, project anxiety, and live plagued by "what ifs" become a part of our subconscious conditioning, thereby creating part of our belief system. Although these are mistaken beliefs, we perceive them as healthy and routinely

---

[3] *Psychological Aspects of Asthma; 10 Years of Research.* September, 2002, Vol. 33, No. 8.

employ them as a way of self-protection and to stay in control. Once this belief is formed in the subconscious, we don't think about initiating anxiety, it's simply done for us! Our racing heart, sweaty palms, and difficulty breathing provide enough evidence to reassure us that there has got to be something wrong, that we are not crazy after all. Even though what we are experiencing are symptoms, we often perceive them as the problem. We can even take this a step further. We can start taking antianxiety medication, which may seem to make things better for a while, reinforcing the belief that there was something wrong, and that the pill is the only thing can help. This kind of belief is common. Unfortunately some of us elevate our anxiety to a level at which we can't function without medication. Anxiety is best neutralized by getting rid of the source and by making the cognitive changes necessary to eliminate repeated negative thought patterns. However, in most cases we can't pinpoint the source. This is not surprising. It's like a mirage—we think you see it, but when we get there it doesn't exist.

The following are some helpful steps to help curb projected anxiety:

1. Check in with your feelings to see if what you are feeling is real fear or if you are checked out to avoid your feelings by projecting.
2. If it's real fear, consider how you are about to get hurt. If it is physical hurt, for example domestic violence, remove yourself from the environment. That fear will turn in to power and self-control. If it is fear of losing someone close to you, don't deny the feeling. Be proactive. Express your fear. Devise an action plan. For example, let's say your best friend is diagnosed with cancer and is in the hospital. Go to the hospital and share your feelings with him so that you don't have any regrets and can ultimately grieve your loss effectively without guilt.
3. If it's false fear or projected anxiety, take a look at what is really going on, what emotions are you running away from subconsciously. Try to identify them so that you can get back into the here and now.

4. Work on changing your mind-set. Realize that it is not the experience of fear that haunts you; it is the interpretation of that experience.
5. Write down and analyze the thought process that is driving your fear, then change it.

Sad

> *There are as many nights as days, and the one is just as long as the other in the year's course. Even a happy life cannot be without a measure of darkness, and the word "happy" would lose its meaning if it were not balanced by sadness.*
>
> —Carl Jung

Feeling sad usually is the result of a sudden, unexpected disappointment in someone or something and also leftover residue from pain. Perhaps we did not get the promotion we were expecting or someone we love left us; in these cases a sad feeling is appropriate. If the sad feeling is very intense, a physical response such as tears is a natural part of the grieving process. Hence without the feeling of sad, grief is not possible. If we experience pain or loss, sadness is the end result of eliminating painful energy. This is why sad is the healing feeling. During the grieving process, we move through various stages of grief but ultimately find comfort and healing in sadness.

However, tears do not necessarily correspond to sadness. For example, someone who is feeling sorry for themselves may cry, but this does not mean they are feeling sad. Although on the surface it appears to be sadness, it may be nothing more than a game of guilt. But those who adopt a "poor me" mentality as a way of facing the world do not necessarily see this guilt as their tears "prove" their sadness. A persistent emotion of sad may turn more into a more pervasive state of sadness in which we feel blue, down, and mildly lethargic. It is a temporary lowering of mood that, if it persists, may lead to depression.

Hurt

"No pain, no gain" is a common phrase. We live in a world where pain and hurt are real. Yet many of us become uncomfortable when we feel hurt and try to avoid pain at all cost. This is especially true for men, especially in certain societies in which it is a sign of weakness for a man to display hurt, and thus unacceptable. Hurt is a difficult feeling to express, especially if we are raised in an emotionally anemic family. The very idea of expressing hurt creates very unsettling feelings in the family system. As a result, our persistent need to distance ourselves from hurt, or deny it, causes us to live a lie and suffer needlessly.

When a child puts his hand on a stove burner and experiences pain, it's that pain that instructs him to pull his hand back. The length of his cry indicates the amount of hurt he sustained. Next time he uses the stove, he will likely avoid touching the burner. Emotional hurt works in much the same manner. When we feel violated or abused by someone, the tendency is to distance ourselves from that person to avoid any future hurt. Hurt is like the wise teacher who lives within us, keeping us from hiding in denial. If we are a good student, our hurt becomes the teacher, and we grow even though it is painful. But if we are student who could not care less, inevitably we will repeat our mistakes, live in constant state of hurt, fail to grow, and become an adult child.

Hurt allows us to establish boundaries with other people because hurt clearly tells us what we will and will not tolerate, assuming we are willing to stand up for what we believe. Failure to defend our hurt leads us to feel repeatedly violated by others. When we fail to take hurt seriously and use it to define ourselves, others will try to define us based upon their selfish reasons. This is why when we undermine our hurt, we undermine ourselves.

All hurt or pain is about a loss, whether the loss of a loved one or the loss of self. When we lose a loved one, the feeling of hurt is overwhelming. Sometimes it even feels as if we have lost a part of ourselves. So we grieve the loss through pain. There is a correlation between the length of grief and the size of the love that we have lost. If the person we lost is a distant family member, we may grieve for a few days, but the hurt is mild and short lived. But if we lose a spouse or a child, the hurt we experience is overwhelming and intense, and our grief may last a lifetime. Although hurt may slowly fade in time, it also serves as a reminder of the love we experienced, which lingers for the rest of our lives. This is why sometimes it hurts to love.

Some of us avoid the grieving process altogether, facing it by taking prescription medications to help us "get through" the grieving process without experiencing much emotion. Feeling this kind of pain is unnatural and uncomfortable. Keeping our composure becomes more important than taking part in the grief process, which may be perceived as emotional weakness. Others of us, who are aware of and comfortable with hurt, do not fear feeling it or expressing it, even though it leaves us vulnerable. However, being vulnerable ultimately becomes strength as it is anchored in honesty.

Loss of self

Loss of self also causes us to feel pain, however, it has nothing to do being numb or getting lost in someone else. It primarily has to do with disowning or violating parts of ourselves, which creates a state of hurt. There are three things we can lose that will cause us to feel loss of self: self-power, control, and self-worth/self-esteem.

Self-Power

When we become the center of our own world, we realize the power we possess to shape our own lives. This power comes from the depths of our soul. It is a free-flowing energy that allows us to empower ourselves as we make decisions based upon our truth and the truth about our feelings. Power to be, power to create, power to love. Imagine you give up this right and allow someone else or something else to have power over you. Losing our own power puts us in a state of hurt.

Feeling powerless, Mary talked about how inadequate she felt in her relationship. She was well-educated and worked at a big company where she managed fifty people, making major decisions throughout the day. However in her relationship, she felt inadequate and doubtful because her husband made most of the decisions. She gradually accepted this as a way of getting along and did not rock the boat. But her resentment grew over time and she started withholding sex from her husband. He in return became more reactive and demanding and occasionally forced her into having sex. Mary's story is a common occurrence in many relationships. When she gave up her power to make peace, the emotion of hurt became her constant friend. As she felt more and more powerless, she reacted with passive anger by withholding sex so that maybe her husband would understand the hurt she is experiencing. Instead of coming from a position of power and taking care of herself, the repressed hurt was masked by her becoming a victim.

The truth is, in relationships where power is at stake, real love and intimacy is not possible.

Control

Control is very important to some of us because it enables us to conceal our weaknesses while appearing self-righteous. Have you ever been in a car with a backseat driver? Although you may be a much better driver, the backseat driver can't help but saying things like, "Put your blinker on" or "Slow down" or "Easy on the brakes." The anger we feel in this situation is a result of the hurt feeling that comes from being overly controlled.

Most of us feel as if we have some sense of control. But the reality is that there is not much we can truly control. And yet, many of us believe that we can control our feelings. For instance, if we are hurt, we may still smile all day long and tell others that we are fine, believing that we are successfully masking our feelings. We come to believe that we have the ability to control our feelings. We may desperately try to manage them by numbing with drugs and alcohol or food, avoiding our feelings as if they are not there, eating to forget. But these fixes are only temporary. Soon we start losing control and come face to face with our repressed emotions. The very thing we are trying to control is actually controlling us. While we cannot control our emotions, we can control how we deal with them.

Self-worth/self-esteem

We live in a world where hurt is inevitable; we can never be totally safe. We may believe that we are a good person and care about other people and how they feel. But inevitably we will come across people who could not care less about us or our emotional well-being. They have only one thing in mind, and that is to emotionally violate others to experience a twisted sense of satisfaction.

During lunch break, Sandra confided in one of her coworkers with whom she thought she was close. She told her coworker that her son was in juvenile hall for burglary and possession of stolen property. She expressed how horrible she felt as a mother. The next day when she walked into work, the receptionist said, "I heard the bad news. I'm so sorry." Shocked and feeling violated, Sandra went to her desk and cried. A month later at a company picnic, Sandra and a couple of her friends decided to play a joke on the coworker who had violated her trust. As Sandra was offering chocolate to everyone, she offered her coworker chocolate that had hot sauce in the middle. Soon after taking a bite from the chocolate, the coworker's face turned red with agony and pain. Sandra and her friends started laughing and explaining the joke to everyone.

When our self-worth and self-esteem is violated by someone calling us a name, or being emotionally abusive, or stabbing us in the back, we feel hurt. Although Sandra was justified in her anger, she didn't understand why she felt so bad after getting even. Because she could not face her emotions honestly, she stooped to her coworker's methods to send a message. What she did not realize is that she was as sick as the person who violated her. When our self-esteem is weak, we become prey for others, allowing them to play with our emotions. No one but ourselves can raise our self-worth. Accepting our feelings without judgment and loving ourselves as we are makes us feel that we are a worthy individual. The best way to protect our self-worth is to believe that we are a good person, and instead of retaliating, elevate ourselves beyond our shortcomings. At that point our feelings will serve us with love, and we can love the person we become.

Anger

> *Holding on to anger is like grasping a hot coal with the intent of throwing it at someone else; you are the one who gets burned.*
>
> —Buddha

Anger is a problematic feeling for many people, and yet anger is really our friend. Many of us don't understand what anger really is, and as a result, feel uncomfortable with feeling it, let alone expressing it. As a result, we perceive anger as a negative emotion. In certain family systems, getting angry or showing anger is not acceptable. Instead, children are rewarded for "being nice" or "acting nice," and showing anger is met with disapproval. The message is sent, and the child learns that the only way he is lovable and acceptable is by being nice. If we grow up learning to perceive anger as a negative and unacceptable emotion, gradually we learn to avoid anger by developing certain defenses and behavioral patterns. This emotional mind-set sets us up as a target for violation, such as molestation, manipulation or ongoing anxiety.

Those of us who grow up in this environment mostly become pleasers, codependent type personalities that are fixated on not upsetting anyone. We become very afraid of getting angry;

afraid we may be rejected for the way we feel. We may become paralyzed in the presence of an angry person, confused and feeling helpless, reacting by trying to stop the angry person from feeling angry by doing anything possible to achieve peace. Because anger and hurt are what allows us to define ourselves by setting limits, we may have a very difficult time defining ourselves as a separate being without getting enmeshed with someone else. This is the primary reason why we may feel responsible for others feelings, thinking that those feelings are our own. The need to do something about the other person's feeling or to fix the situation becomes imperative.

In family systems in which a child is subjected to rage, domestic violence, etc., the child starts to perceive that all human relationships are about acting out, violation, shame, and blame. So he adopts acting out as a normal way of relating to others and a way of processing anger. Soon he starts driving the family into chaos by being reactive, seeking negative attention to be noticed, setting in motion the belief system that the one who is loudest gets heard the most and that world is an angry place. As the person gets older, the core shame of being rejected and feeling worthless is increasingly defended by anger. As shame grows, so does the amount of anger. Out of fear of being exposed, he will use his anger when needed to deter anyone from getting close while masking his shame at the same time. As he realizes the power of his anger, he utilizes it effectively to dominate others into submission in order to feel some sense of control. Ultimately this person recreates a world of chaos and conflict—the very thing he was trying to get away from as a child.

The best way to process anger is to pinpoint the origin of the pain. It is a powerful and effective way of processing anger without acting out. But the problem with anger is that it is often not anger but rather unidentified hurt. Hence, we experience the energy negatively, and then feel the need to act out verbally by raising our voices, screaming, or resorting to a physical display such as punching holes in the walls or breaking things. When we can't identify our emotional pain, the need to resolve it becomes an overwhelming need for some by turning to physical acting out.

These acts give us the impression that the anger is now out of our system. Some of the adolescents I have treated have acted their anger out by punching holes in the walls (some even punched brick walls!), often causing themselves physical damage and prolonged pain. When I asked them how they felt afterward, the most common response was, "I felt much better." When we can't figure out the source of our emotional pain, we may turn it into physical pain by self-mutilation such as cutting. This enables us to finally identify with the pain and externalize it.

Another misconception about the anger process is that it is helpful to hit a punching bag or engage in repeated physical activity such weight lifting to the point of injury. It's inevitable that we will be exhausted at the end of such physical act, however, this physical exhaustion does not mean the anger is now out of our system. Our emotional body is designed to process emotional energy—it is a mistaken belief that we can resolve negative emotional energy through physical means. Unless we learn to get in touch with our pain and anger and learn to process it without negative consequences, the outcome will always disappoint us.

Anger Management

Are you managing anger or your anger is managing you? Experiencing anger is easy, but managing anger is a different story. Many of us have anger issues. Not realizing that anger is old pain, many of us try to find ways to deal with our anger. Some of us take, or are forced into, classes to resolve anger due to legal problems such as charges of domestic abuse.

Assume for a moment that you are a pan of boiling milk. Milk is your anger, the flame is the event or issue that incited it, and the pan represents your body. After a while, as the milk temperature rises (you build up emotion inside and your energy level rises), the milk starts forming big bubbles that come to the surface. Your options are let it boil over, move the pan away from the heat and let it cool off for a while before returning it to the heat, or turning the heat off completely. Unfortunately, since most of us don't know how to turn the heat off, we usually choose the cool-off-then-heat-up process. When we do this, we become moody and often out of control. Because nobody knows when we are going to boil over, people around us always seem to walking on egg shells. We may learn some skills to calm our anger, such as breathing, counting backward, or going outside to get some fresh air.

One evening, Jim started an argument over his wife coming home late. Soon he started screaming and punched a hole in the wall. Realizing that he had violated a court order and was jeopardizing his marriage, he decided to go for a drive to cool off. After a half-hour drive, he started feeling much better. As he turned around and started heading back home, another driver cut in front of him by mistake. Jim started yelling profanities, caught up with the other car, and drove the driver off the road. After his arrest, his wife asked him what happened. He said he didn't do anything wrong—it was the other driver's fault that he got arrested.

When we adopt new behaviors to stop the emotional hurt and anger, we simply postpone the inevitable. Unless we come to terms with our core hurt and anger, every small present anger is going to summon many repressed emotions from our past which inevitably make us boil over. As we keep repeating this self-destructive act, we start perceiving ourselves as a failure, burdened with guilt about our behavior or the pain we have caused others. Feeling remorseful, we make promises over and over that it will never happen again. But our anger will never bargain with our promises.

Rage

Whatever is begun in anger ends in shame.

—Benjamin Franklin

Rage is a primitive form of anger. When we do not develop healthy anger, we may resort to rage as a form of anger management. Rage is like an active volcano. It has erupted before and caused emotional and physical devastation. In between eruptions, we see small amounts of smoke seeping through the cracks, keeping us on pins and needles, wondering when the next explosion will occur. Rage, like anger, engulfs us with an instant overwhelming negative energy, an outburst just like the volcano. In a way, living with someone who rages is just like living next to a volcano. Unresolved anger constantly seeks to be discharged. But anger, often triggered by a symbolic emotional event, builds to unacceptable energy levels. The sudden discharge of this energy prevents us from considering the possible devastating consequences of our reactions. It is almost like being in brief psychotic state. Think of every unresolved or repressed feeling of anger as an individual link in a chain. With every act of repressing anger we create a new link. As we get older, the chain grows and grows until we eventually reach the saturation point. From this point on, every new anger-producing event acts triggers all of the repressed anger, causing a chain reaction that results in a rage episode.

Some of the people I have treated for rage disorders have described their rage experience as feeling as if they are in a tunnel, covered with dark gray clouds, unable to hear or recall what anyone said. In some cases, they strongly denied what they did while in a rage. Rage is primarily about fear and control. On the surface, someone in a rage appears to be unapproachable, scary, and distant. Their threatening demeanor or often physically challenging behaviors are designed to hide the secret that they are scared inside. They learned that the act of rage deters anyone from getting emotionally close them. Their outward expression regarding relationships is that they can take it or leave it while they are yearning for love and nurturing deep within. As a result, these people often form superficial ties and show very little interest in their partners.

The basic premise of rage is that we mask our fears by making others fear us. A dictator can achieve the same goal on a bigger scale. Hitler is a good example of this. In a short period of time, he was able to rule the country by establishing total intimidation and fear over everyone. Killing innocent people was simply an ongoing reinforcement of fear and justification for his rage. The other aspect of rage is control. Although control is an illusion, someone who rages learns one thing quickly: the act of rage repels people, often paralyzing and intimidating them. It makes people stay away. This gives the rager the illusion of control as well as false sense of power. He realizes the power of control and how he can manipulate his environment as well as the people in it. Rage is also a physiological event. When all the repressed anger is release all at once in the form of rage, the body produces a hormone called adrenaline. Adrenaline is the hormone that is primarily responsible for fight-and-flight response. The repeated act of rage is directly correlated to the amount of adrenaline produced in every act. Someone who rages starts seeking that feeling of released adrenaline when they rage. You may have heard the term "adrenaline junkie." Evil Kenevil described the feeling of an intense high or rush as he was jumping over eighteen school buses on his motorcycle. Someone who rages can indeed achieve the same state to a lesser degree, and it's very addictive. It's not a coincidence that people often rage over seemingly irrelevant things or seek out arguments.

Guilt

Guilt is regret for what we've done
Regret is guilt for what we didn't do.
—Casey

When anger gets bottled up and turned against the self it leads to guilt. The inability to deal with anger effectively along with a shame-based belief system makes guilt a complicated feeling. Generally when we make a mistake, we immediately feel badly and judge ourselves because we have been judged (or expect to be judged) by others. This judging reinforces what we believe about ourselves. "I made a mistake" becomes "I am a mistake." This is one of the reasons most people can't separate guilt from shame. As we continue through life, a shame-based belief becomes an inescapable outcome. In order to deal with guilt effectively, we have to be willing to see if the guilt is the result of repressed anger or due to a mistake. If it's due to anger, it must be dealt with as anger. If it's due to a mistake, it must be dealt with as embarrassment. For this reason, I prefer to use the concept of "embarrassed" instead of "guilt."

A very shy guy goes into a bar and sees a beautiful woman sitting at the bar. After an hour of gathering up his courage, he finally walks over to her and asks tentatively, "Um, would you mind if I chatted with you for a while?" She responds by yelling at the top of her lungs, "No! I won't sleep with you tonight!" Everyone in the bar is now staring at them. Naturally, the guy is hopelessly embarrassed and slinks back to his table. After a few minutes, the woman walks over to him and apologizes. She smiles at him and says, "I'm sorry if I embarrassed you. You see, I'm a graduate student in psychology and I'm studying how people respond to embarrassing situations." To which he responds at the top of his lungs, "What do you mean $200?"

Embarrassment can be a transforming feeling if it is rooted in the spiritual body in the form of remorse. Without remorse there is no deeper understanding of our humanness and our shortcomings. Remorse, like compassion, is experienced at higher levels of consciousness while guilt is experienced in the habitual existence of the subconscious. This is primary while so many people don't know how to be humble; they don't feel remorse but instead beat themselves up with guilt. Humility makes us down-to-earth resulting in complete self-acceptance while guilt repeatedly promotes self-rejection.

Guilt and shame are two different ways of being and seeing the world. For some of us, there is no difference between guilt and shame, hence when we feel guilt we feel shame. Deep within we feel guilty as charged. This self-judgment triggers our core shame, which we carry as a banner for the rest of our lives. When we admit we made a mistake and take ownership for that mistake, we are not in denial. We see ourselves as we are, without any distortions. Hence, we are less likely to repeat our mistakes—we see them as teachers. Guilt, on the other hand, leads us to a sense of "poor me," feelings of worthlessness, and throwing pity parties that no one wants to attend. Guilt is a human emotion; animals do not experience guilt.

One day I watched a cat in my backyard fixated on a bird. The bird was busy feeding itself and was not aware of the cat. The cat crept toward the bird as if in slow-motion. This went on for a while until the cat came near enough that the bird flew away. Following that event, the cat laid on the grass, licking her paws, relaxed in the sun. If the cat was a human being, what would be his reaction? He would probably say things like, "I can't believe I couldn't catch that bird!" or "It figures, I knew I was not going to get that bird" or maybe "I didn't really want to catch that bird anyway."

Those of us who are guilty tend to be primarily negative and live in a negative world. In that world we operate out of self-hatred and rejection. Along the way we realize the power of guilt and how we can manipulate others with it. Along the way we master how to play the victim role with our loved ones when it's convenient for us to achieve the desired outcome. Exaggerating our emotions, especially hurt, we project an image of hopelessness in order to get favors. We often appeal to other people's pity by creating the image of a helpless person. We realized long ago that, by making others to feel sorry for us, we can be rescued.

When those of us who are guilty realize how we can control others with guilt, it may become part of our lifetime mission to meet our emotional and physical needs on a continual basis. Not at all concerned with how we impact others around us, our narcissistic needs become a priority. Those of us who are guilty are unable to give out of love since there is so little we feel deep within ourselves. As a result, we give with conditions and we expect a return. Very often we remind others how we sacrificed for them or what we gave them to keep them subservient to our guilt. When we are in a relationship with someone, we may coerce them into doing things out of guilt or obligation, rendering them merely a hostage. We may expect things to go our way in order to feel good and remain in control of the situation, and if someone crosses us, we may retreat into self-pity. Tears become our ultimate control mechanism. Crying as we retreat into helplessness, we project an image of a little child who is out in the cold, shivering, waiting to be rescued. If this fails, we may switch to a cold shoulder and silence down the road as we try to manipulate others into achieving our desired outcome.

Lily said, "Christmas is not a fun time in our family. As a child I don't recall a fun Christmas. There was always drama and conflict. Someone getting drunk and creating a scene was the norm. After I got married, I was expected to have Christmas dinner at my house. Every year I woke up before everyone to start the cooking and get everything ready. As family members came, I was expected to greet them and socialize while making sure everything was going well in the kitchen. Year after year my mom always found something wrong with my cooking and talked about how hers tasted so much better. After they left, I was up late cleaning. One year, feeling exhausted, used, and unappreciated, I decided to tell my mom that the next Christmas dinner should be at her house. As my mom complained about how Dad will be disappointed, and that her shoulder is bothering her, and that she is in pain, I found myself feeling guilty and accepting the situation. As this Christmas neared, I found myself having anxiety attacks, unable to sleep. I knew something was wrong with me. I had a phone conversation with my mom two weeks ago; I told her how I am suffering and that I might need some counseling. She replied, "I don't know what is going on with you. I for sure did not raise you this way. You don't need any help—only crazy people do."

I'm sure similar stories play out in many homes. Because of past experiences, we may not want to attend certain parties or gatherings. But each time, we are unable to say no to the invitation due to our own guilt about possibly hurting or upsetting others. So we dread going, and once we get there we become pretentious, uneasy and can't wait to leave. However, we feel angry and disappointed in ourselves after leaving. We may say to ourselves, "Never again!" Our inability to be honest with ourselves, respect our emotions, and take an honest position gives way to guilt over time, and we end up repeating the very behavior we resent. Our need for self-punishment is left unexamined as we are too busy shifting blame onto others to avoid looking at ourselves.

CHAPTER 7 *Stress and Depression*

> *Stress is nothing more than a socially acceptable form of disease.*
> —R. Carlson

Stress

Are you stressed? What are you doing about it? We all experience stress in varying forms and degrees every day. In small doses, stress can actually be beneficial to us. Sometimes the source from which stress originates is clear. Stress is inevitable when we are faced with life-changing events such as divorce, loss of employment, the death of a loved one, or having a baby. However, other times we may not know why we feel stressed. This is normal. However, some of us live in a state of perpetual stress. Anyone who is subjected to ongoing stress for an extended period will likely suffer emotional, physical, and medical problems. Stress is like a rust that gradually starts accumulating on the surface of an iron when the environmental conditions are just right. If further neglected, the iron will corrode eventually to the point of breaking.

Stress lets us know that something is not right, that we are not at ease, that we are "dis-eased." As the negative emotions bottle up, just like the rust accumulates on the iron, our stressed system becomes fragile and vulnerable to any threat. Many of us are poorly equipped to deal with stress simply because we don't know what stress is and how to manage it. We perceive stress based upon what is happening around us, the kind of events we are experiencing. If we are fighting with our spouse, or having financial problems, we feel stressed and we believe that if the problem goes away, the stress will end. When the situation changes, we may feel some relief, but then something else seems to pop up, and we are back to being stressed.

Stress is the end result of unexpressed emotions related to those events we are experiencing. When our emotional body is burdened with stress, our physical body responds chemically by producing the cortisol hormone, which engages the body in a protection mode. This hormone is so powerful that, as an example, a pregnant mom sends messages to the fetus through this hormone that change the character of the developing child's physiology (Lesage et. al., 2004; Christensen, 2000; and Arnsten, 1998). (need full citation)

As our society becomes more complex, increasing levels of stress are becoming the norm. It is becoming an acceptable way of life to make a living at the expense of our health and well-being. Although some aspects of life are becoming increasingly unhealthy, such as unacceptable levels of toxins in the water, daily radiation exposure, and unhealthy air quality, we are expected to accept and adjust and pretend it doesn't matter. As stress becomes more of a hidden societal disease, the changes in attitudes, behaviors, and debilitating health consequences become simply a way of adjusting to it.

How often does a feeling come to the surface as a response to an experience and you hold it in because another person might be injured or may not like you expressing it? You may not want to offend the other person but more likely you don't want to running the risk of him not liking your current feeling and rejecting you.

The truth is that we always pay the price of allowing ourselves to be inhibited from our rightful expression. When we don't take the emotional risk to express what is inside of us, we suffer. Stress is the pressure of unexpressed emotions. Many of us live in this state, accepting this as a way of life and feeling as if there is nothing we can do about it. Ultimately, prolonged stress leads to depression or a nervous breakdown.

Life follows a certain logical pathway. We are standing right in the middle of it, the creator of our own path. Where we go from here no one knows, but while we are on this journey we must be honest about our feelings; expressing them so that they do not take down the present with past experiences, causing us to experience them over and over, eventually feeling emotionally overwhelmed and stressed. To distress, we must express.

Depression

> *A doctor says to his wife,*
> *Cancer is a funny thing*
> *Childless women get it*
> *Men when they retire*
> *As if they had to be an outlet*
> *For their foiled creative fire.*
> —W. H. Auden

We all thrive when our creative energy is channeled through us. We experience fulfillment and joy. Losing this positive energy can be a gradual process such as bottling up negative emotions or experiencing a sudden meaningful loss. Previously I described trying to push a beach ball underwater and how much energy it takes to keep it submerged. This constant battle of protecting ourselves from negative emotions not only isolates the emotions but our whole selves from the world. As guilt, pain, and anger drain our rightful positive energy from us, we gradually lose the ability to bottle these emotions up. This loss of energy and lack of motivation are symptoms of depression.

As we sink into depression, our belief system reacts with total agreement, reinforcing our feelings of being worthless and undeserving. As we direct our anger and guilt toward ourselves, this self-hatred reinforces the punishment we think we deserve. Reality becomes painful, and as the pain and sadness becomes unbearably overwhelming, we may look for a desperate way out in order to stop the emotions, such as suicide.

Most of the time, loved ones do not understand depression. They reach out by saying things like, "Why don't you just snap out of it!" or desperately trying to do things to get us out of our depressive state. Unless we are able to break the self-destructive cycle by letting out our emotions, we will continue to suffer. We may require professional medical intervention as well as therapy to work through trapped emotions. Recognizing the event(s) that caused us to bottle up all of the emotions is a great place to start. However, if we are severely depressed, this by itself is not enough.

In many instances, life may seem to be going fine until some event causes unexpected loss or pain, such as losing a partner, a child, or a job. Many of us are not equipped to deal with such overwhelming pain, which puts us into a state of depression. Depression may surface gradually or be an instant reaction.

Joe talked about his loss of his father. When he found out that his dad had a terminal cancer and did not have much time left, he went to see a psychiatrist and got some tranquilizers to get through these difficult times. On the day of his dad's death and during the funeral, he did not feel much of anything, and things seemed to go well for a while. When I asked him approximately when his depression started, his answer was after his father's death. As Joe realized how he avoided his father's death by denying that pain of loss, only then was he able to give himself permission to get angry and cry and ultimately come to terms with his loss.

Depression is quite common among adolescents as they navigate a constant battle with their sense of self-worth and self-esteem. Unfortunately, for some elderly people, depression is an inevitable end because they lived their lives denying their feelings. One thing is clear, as people reach their golden years, their defenses start crumbling, and they can no longer deny the truth about who they are, what they have become, or the regrets they may have about their lives. For some, loss of purpose leads to depression. Resolving depression requires figuring out what emotions have created it.

CHAPTER 8 — *How to Process Feelings*

> *Sometimes when I say, "Oh don't worry, I'm fine . . ." I just want someone, once, to look me in the eyes and just say "Don't. Tell the truth."*
> —Anonymous

When we have a feeling that comes to the surface as a response to an experience, how often do we withhold that feeling? Why do we do this? The following are some common beliefs:

- If I express my feelings, I may hurt or cause harm to others. Many of us carry this belief due to inadequacies based on family secrets and social conditioning. Think for a moment about what this statement really means. Do we *really* have the power to *hurt* someone by expressing true feelings in a proper manner? No. We may, however, hurt someone's feeling by expressing our feelings with the intent to retaliate, violate, or abuse others, overstating our pain to humiliate and get even. It is important to express feelings with the proper intent.

- Feelings can't be expressed at work or in social situations.

Carrie went to her supervisor and stated that a coworker had been making sexual jokes that make her feel uncomfortable. The supervisor responded by stating that he didn't believe the joker meant anything by it and that Carrie should not take it personally. Six months later, Carrie filed a lawsuit against the company. The supervisor was shocked and reacted with anger, accusing Carrie of seeking easy money.

The idea of feelings in the workplace sounds awkward because we have developed a belief that both cannot coexist. This mind-set is one of the reasons why many organizations develop a dysfunctional culture. Feelings in the workplace do not mean discussing our marital problems with coworkers at work, but rather expressing our feelings about work and our work environment. Most workplaces are stressful to some degree, and it is inevitable that personality conflicts occur. These conflicts greatly affect employee attitudes and productivity. We have established a mind-set that work and feelings do not mix, and therefore we are forced to be "human doings" under the pretense of professionalism, creating an unhealthy work personality.

As a society, we learn to greet each other based upon our social conditioning and obligation by asking questions such as, "How are you?" and "What's up?" and responding "I'm good" or "Just fine" even when we may be hurting inside. The painful truth is that people in general are not interested in how you are doing, let alone how you are feeling. Hence, work is work, and we become an extension of that piece of work. The same consequences of repressing feelings described previously apply to repressing feelings at work; we can't leave our feelings at home, and therefore the struggle with the self is an inevitable outcome. The more we try to pretend, the more likely we will experience feelings of alienation and job burnout. When we fear expressing the truth, we don't feel safe, just as some of us felt in early childhood. Fear of punishment or retaliation causes us to keep our distance in the workplace, and as a result, the environment becomes in cohesive. It is inevitable that resentful employees become less productive, gossip, isolate, and use sick days frequently. On the other hand, when we treat each other with kindness, respect, and are comfortable in the workplace, we become much more productive. Establishing an emotionally healthy work environment must start at the top level and be properly modeled to the rest of the organization.

- Expressing feelings is a sign of weakness. This stems from cultural conditioning, which tends to equate lack of emotion with strength. Because strength is traditionally a masculine characteristic, many men are uncomfortable expressing feelings.

The fact is that we always pay a price for inhibiting our core feelings. We are led to believe that we must become a different person in certain social situations as if we are chameleons. We must behave like everyone else does, say what others want to hear or what is acceptable. This pressure to be other than who we are is stressful.

For example, why can we not respond honestly when somebody at work asks us how we are today? Why can we not say, "Actually, I'm kind of sad today?" The reason such an honest response often results in discomfort is that we often don't stop there but go further to elaborate on why we are feeling sad. This serves no purpose. Remember the importance of taking feelings to the source that caused them and releasing them there. Most people, especially coworkers, really do not care about our feelings; only those who love and care for us may have some interest in understanding our feelings and their source. Others, when faced with this information, may judge us or worse, use it against us. So we can be true to ourselves by simply answering the question "How are you?" with a simple, honest response, such as "I'm a little sad today." Answering honestly anchors us in truth and makes us a better person.

Here is a great way of practicing. One day at work, respond to each inquiry as to how you are doing by saying, "I'm fine, how are you?" As you can imagine, your coworkers will say they are great and move on. The next day, try to answer as you honestly feel. For example, "I'm kind of sad today, how are you?" You will likely get questioned about why you are sad. Simply respond, "I'm just sad, that's all" and move on. You will feel wonderful because you will no longer be responding based on fear of social acceptance.

Life is happening at this very moment and so are our feelings. If we want to be free of negative emotions then we must take learn to risk of sharing feelings as they happen in the present. True commitment to our feelings serves us with kindness and rewards us with boundless emotional self mastery.

Feelings enhance memory—how we actually encode and consolidate different pieces of information, especially information that is especially salient. We can't just wish feelings away or try to forget them—it's like trying to separate milk from cheese. They are one. But we can free ourselves from feelings that cause us suffering by doing the following:

1. Identify the core feeling(s)—Identify what you are feeling deep within you whether it is anger, sad, happy, hurt, afraid, or guilt (embarrassed). There is no limit as to how many feelings you can feel at any given time. What you feel is correct for that moment. Remember feelings do not choose you, you choose them. Make sure the feeling you get in touch with is your true feeling, not what you *think* you should feel. Failure to identify your feelings will cause you to feel doubt, confusion and lead you down the wrong path.
2. Identify who or what is causing you to feel this way—Once you identify the feeling(s), try to pinpoint who or what caused those feelings. Getting face-to-face with the source will ignite your feelings and enable you to easily get in touch with them. When you shy away from the source of your anger, you will most likely act it out or misdirect your anger. For instance, if your boyfriend hurt you and you call your friend to tell her about it, you may seem to experience some temporary relief, but your feelings are still trapped deep within. You simply recycled your feelings and will continue to do so if you avoid the source of your pain.
3. Express, express, express—Once you identify the feeling(s) and the source, expressing that feeling in a timely

manner will set you free. Direct appropriate expression of feelings is a must for healthy emotional life. Confront both the feeling(s) and the source openly. Remember the example of trying to force the beach ball into the pool, and how energy-consuming that is? Instead, let it go in the direction it needs to go. Stop being a hostage to the emotion that has been draining you, going against your basic nature. Instead, flow with the natural process of that energy. Here's how to do it:

DO . . .

- Make sure you are in touch with the true primary feeling you are about to express.

- Make sure you are not blaming, shaming or attacking.

- Ask the source of your emotion just to listen, and tell him that you are not there to argue.

- Start with "I feel hurt, angry, etc."

- Keep eye contact.

- Get your message across in less than fifteen seconds.

- Allow the feelings go through you.

DON'T . . .

- Modify your natural core feelings in order to accommodate others (e.g., "I am confused" or "I am frustrated")—these are not core feelings. "I feel that . . ." is not the same as "I feel sad . . ." Statements such as "I feel that things are not going well between us" gives the illusion that you are expressing true feelings.

- Look down, up, cover your face, etc. The true empowerment comes from facing your feelings in the face of another person. Remember, the eyes are the window to the soul.

- Do not give a dissertation. If you feel the need to talk and repeat or explain the problem, you are cycling, which will only result in more anger and frustration.

- Set clear, firm limits and boundaries; changing them simply sends the other person a clear message that "I am not what I say I am, so ignore what I established before." Limits are like white picket fences—they define us and give us a sense of autonomy. Limits are set based upon our emotional needs and knowing what hurts us. Set realistic limits that you are willing to enforce, otherwise the other person will perceive your limits as empty threats and soon become numb to them. When what we say and what we do not complement each other, we live in a world of pain and perpetual disappointment. Some limits may change because our wants and needs change. But others, such as "I will not tolerate adultery," are constant. Some people will respect our boundaries while others could not care less about them. After setting limits, we must follow through—removing those who continue to disrespect them from our lives or removing ourselves from the situation. If we don't protect our own limits, why should anyone else respect them?

Fear holds us back from being honest with our feelings because the possibility of being humiliated or rejected feels very real. But when we learn to express our feelings, we empower ourselves and fear can no longer silence us. Nobody is perfect, but inside each of us there is perfect sense of ourselves waiting to become, a notion of a better us yearning to take over. We are waiting to be there for ourselves. The person inside us knows when things are right. All we need to be is our right selves, our honest selves, and our true selves.

Magical Thinking

A common mistake when learning to process feelings is to believe that, immediately after expressing an emotion, we will feel great and the discomfort will completely dissipate. This is not so. Think of your feelings as being trapped in a champagne bottle which you shake and shake and finally uncork. While a large amount of the champagne sprays out of the bottle, some champagne remains. So is with our emotional body. As negative emotions build, so does the pressure of that negative energy. As we start releasing that specific feeling in the present, our emotional body responds by eliminating some of the other similar negative emotions at the same time. Once our emotional pathways are open to their natural course, the remaining emotions will work themselves out of our system as we become readily available to our feelings in the present.

Grief is a natural process, but we must allow our emotional body some time to work through it. We need to be able to adjust and accept the changes as they occur instead of holding on to specific expectations of how we imagined it to be, which only leads to disappointment and regret. We need to stay out of the way of our emotional body's natural grieving process, trusting that it is there to serve us and that it has the ability to heal our broken heart.

Trust Your Intuition or "gut feelings"

Intuition is nothing more than an expression of your real self. It is a sense of knowing, based on feelings, that comes from the experience rather than from analysis. But intuition can be distorted by the needs arising from feelings that have not been expressed, feelings that have not been identified and sources that have not been made clear. Only when we come from a position of self-acceptance can our intuition be clear enough to be perceived without distortion, and therefore, be trustworthy.

The knowledge we acquire at school is of limited value unless applied properly. But the knowledge that comes from an open heart is ours for the taking, requiring only that we pay attention to what we feel. Our intuition can tell us things far beyond what our mind can perceive. Listen closely to your intuition and allow it to make judgments for you. The best managers follow their intuition and trust, against the odds; their belief in something makes it happen.

Road Blocks to Emotional Self Mastery

As I grew up, I became my own biggest hurdle.
—Casey

What is preventing you from creating the life you desire? The things that we believe stand in our way are obstacles because we make them obstacles. While we may feel anger at times because of these perceived obstacles, on a subconscious level we are comfortable with them. We often allow things to obstruct our goals because we don't think we deserve to reach our goals. These obstructions keep us from testing just how strong and worthy we really are. It is common for people who are seeking to be financially wealthy to first look at the road blocks that prevent them from moving forward. Achieving emotional self mastery requires the same process, although the results are ultimately more fulfilling because we are investing in ourselves.

The Role of Intellect

Recognizing a problem is only the first step toward solving it; understanding its emotional makeup is necessary to solve the problem.

True intelligence comes from knowing thyself emotionally. Feelings are the way we communicate with ourselves, but instead, we use our intellect to try to explain them. A thought is a period of thinking and increased attention. While some thoughts do not carry any feeling, for example, the fact that two plus two equals four, many thoughts and feelings are intertwined. Some thoughts generate feelings. For example, we may start thinking about someone who has died, which leads to a feeling of loss. Conversely, some feelings can make us think. For example, we may be watching a movie about war that makes us cry, which may lead to thinking about the concept of war.

Early in life, we learned and memorized a great deal of information, such as dates of certain events and mathematical formulas. When we turn on our computer, we use our intellect and memory to perform the function. When the screen lights up, do we jump up and down with happiness? Of course not. The act of turning on the computer is a basic function of intellect that does not have any emotion attached to it. But if the computer crashes, do we tell ourselves it's only logical that computers crash from time to time and walk away with a smile? Or do we experience anger and frustration? Why do we have two different reactions to two similar processes associated with the same object? Because, even though we are doing something intellectual, our reaction to a given event is clearly emotional, which ignores logic.

Intelligent people do not have any advantage over less intelligent people when it comes to understanding and processing feelings. It does not make any difference how many degrees one has or how intelligent one is; feelings cannot be processed by intellect. In fact, intellect can be a hindrance as it may lead to trying to explain life instead of experiencing the emotion of it, focusing on justifying the outcome to make some sense of an emotionally anemic world.

Jeff, a brilliant English Professor, revealed in therapy that his last girlfriend left him after seven months. He believed the relationship was going well, although his girlfriend had expressed occasional dissatisfaction. He described the relationship very eloquently, almost like a well-written novel. It seemed as if he was describing someone else's relationship. When I asked about his past relationships, he reported that he had been in six relationships over the past ten years, most of which were ended by his various partners. He said that his relationships started well, as women seem to be drawn to him initially, but that the relationships soon lost their magic. In each case, he identified specific reasons for the deterioration. When I asked him what reasons his partners gave for leaving him, he replied, "They said that I'm not emotionally available." When I asked him if he agreed with their analysis, he continued to explain the reasons why each relationship could not have worked. Jeff was masterful at justifying the failed relationships and manipulating the conversation. He knew that he could always count on his superior intelligence to provide the "right" answers to every question. But what he didn't know is that his intellect, the very thing that he was proud of, was contributing to his loneliness.

Many intelligent people are so far removed from their feelings that they are unable to form healthy relationships, whether between a parent and a child or a romantic relationship. Instead of connecting emotionally, feelings of distrust and distancing become the common bond. A common theme among intellectual people is that they learned very early on not to feel or rely on feelings because of childhood trauma, an emotionless family environment, or improper mirroring by parents. The response to such existence is the defense of intelligence. They learn quickly how to make some sense of their world or the events by using their intelligence as a tool to help them survive the pain by avoiding the feeling. Their intellect becomes their trustworthy friend, providing them a safe, though limiting place from which to operate.

Once the intellect turns into a form of defense called intellectualization/justification, then the person often operates from this defensive point of view.

    diagram of intellect alone vs. intellect + feelings *(to follow)*

Feeling always precedes thought; thought is always an explanation of feeling. Therefore, thoughts are basically an indirect way of dealing with the world. Everything in the end turns out to be a feeling in our system. Many of us get caught in analysis paralysis. Even a simple matter becomes an ongoing chatter in our brain.

To make matters worse, when we try to sleep, we can't seem to stop the brain from overanalyzing the day's events, tomorrow's calendar, etc. We perceive this pervasive sense of uneasiness and stress as a normal way of life without understanding the true impact on us. Overanalyzing is a way to compensate for an inability get in touch with and express feelings. Our world is complex and requires complexity to process it. When we evaluate incoming stimuli from the narrow spectrum of an intellectual band, as opposed to the full range of intellect and emotion, it is unsettling.

In many cases, our feelings can come to the rescue, helping us face powerful stimuli without having to go through a complex mental process that ultimately ends in the same conclusion. For example, if we are woken from a deep sleep by the smell of smoke, an immediate emotion of fear gets us quickly out of the house. If instead we were to lie there and analyze the situation, we would clearly reach the same conclusion that we needed to get out of the house! However, if we were to spend a great deal of time analyzing instead of acting, we might be unable to achieve the desired result. The more emphasis we put on intellectual processing, the less likely we are to use common sense. Ultimately, it is being in touch with this experiential knowledge that enables us to evolve and reach our true potential as this knowledge is transformational, life-changing, and permanent.

Excessive Talk and Need to Over-explain

Another way to compensate for the inability to express feelings is excessive talk and over-explanation. For example, when a simple statement such as "I am hurt" will suffice, we may feel compelled to explain and justify why we are entitled to feel hurt. Often, we do this without realizing it because it feels natural to talk for extended periods of time. But when we are unable to express feelings, it often results in the issue becoming exaggerated and confused. A simple statement evolves into storytelling, and we may get lost along the way. This confusion frequently results in the storyteller saying, "So where was I?" Storytelling is a way to avoid feelings and an attempt to try to release feelings through stories. While it's typically exhausting to talk for a long time, we may come to believe that doing so is the ultimate way to relieve negative energy. Gossiping and reading tabloids fall into this area. Those of us who enjoy these activities are more comfortable focusing on others and their problems, while our built-in judgment mechanism subconsciously allows us to compare and contrast our feelings against those of others. By pinpointing the worst aspects of others, we are able to temporarily avoid our own shortcomings. Since our ego is what we think we are, taking inventory of others and finding faults in them enables us to boost our ego by experiencing an exaggerated sense of self and feeling good short-term.

Consider this workplace dialogue:

Suzie: Did you hear Janet is pregnant?

Jane: I did not know that. Are you sure?

Suzie: That's what I hear. What's even worse is that it may not even be her boyfriend's kid! That wouldn't surprise me—they haven't been getting along for a while. I saw roses on her desk the other day, and I doubt they were from her boyfriend—he's too cheap to send flowers.

Have you ever had a conversation with someone who talks about a personal matter and just when you think they are done, they start explaining the same thing from a different point of view or using a new example, even though you already clearly understood where they are coming from? Sometimes people will keep talking and talking until you stop them or simply tune them out. This is a symptom of fear of abandonment. People who have a fear of abandonment believe that expressing feelings may cause the person to whom they are talking to feel uneasy, or perhaps even reject them, so they believe that it is safer to explain the issue in detail from different points of view. If the person to whom they are talking says, "I heard you, please stop," they will often respond, "Oh, OK. I was just making sure you understood what I was saying." It is very important to be understood. While they are busy making sure that they are understood, the person to whom they are speaking has already shut down or checked out to escape the relentless verbal beating (death by lecture). If the person to whom they are speaking does not respond favorably or interrupts, they feel unheard and rejected and are likely to retreat into self-pity. Hence, they create drama, which becomes their way of acting out their feelings.

Drama allows us to live our emotions "on a stage of the world" rather than process them. It's very much like an actor studying a script and then gradually becoming the person whose role he is acting; beginning to act out emotions knowing that they are not his. Once the act is over, he moves on to the next act. Those of us who adopted drama as a way of acting out emotions see the world as the stage on which we further shape our identity.

The Question of Why?

Many of us believe that if we can find an answer to the question of "Why?" we will have an "Aha!" moment that will bring clarity, but it just doesn't happen. Yet we continue to spend energy trying to find out why something happened or why we feel the way we do rather than just simply accepting what is. Many of us believe that if we can figure out the "why," the pain will magically diminish or disappear. But this is a myth. It is magical thinking.

If we ask someone who has been through years of psychoanalysis what they have gained from it, they may say that they have a better understanding of what went wrong in a relationship or may have learned more about themselves, but they are often more confused and still unable to reach a state of contentment. Those who spend years analyzing everything without the help of psychoanalysis are likely to feel even more burdened and confused. Trying to make sense of feelings with intellect is like trying to unlock a dead bolt with a screw driver—eventually we may be successful at unlocking the lock, but think about the amount of energy and frustration and time that it took to achieve the desired result! Although we have achieved the desired outcome, we are still not likely to feel happy or content because when something becomes a chore (doing something out of obligation or guilt), it is no longer worth having. There is a direct correlation between the quest to answer "why" and intellectualization—both approaches keep us "in our head."

Suzanne, a thirty-six-year-old mother of two, caught her husband having an affair with his secretary. Although this was a very painful ordeal for her, her primary focus was on answering the question, "Why did he do this to me?" Even after her husband left her a letter stating that he didn't love her anymore, she still sought an answer to the same question. After I pointed out that her husband's letter answered that question, she replied, "But why doesn't he love me anymore? I thought everything was fine."

Ultimately, we must accept that is not important to know why we feel the way we do. What is important is to understand what we are feelings we attach or, what they mean to us, and ultimately to be able to act on those feelings. This is where real understanding and insight lies.

Remembering the Past/Opening a Can of Worms

Events and experiences in our memory fade with time. As adults, we may respond to an event very differently than we would have as a child since we are better equipped to deal with stressors. In early childhood, painful experiences such as abandonment and abuse are met with strong denial based on self-preservation. Nevertheless, the painful events and the feelings are recorded in our subconscious. The more we deny the event, the more convoluted it becomes when the time comes to recall it. Because of this, most of the feelings that are attached to these events become distorted. Sometimes some of these feelings surface unattached to events. Unattached feelings, scattered deep within our subconscious, may surface when we experience similar feelings as the result of a different event. That new event, then, becomes the new home for the unattached emotion as well. This is largely due to the work of our subconscious mind's need to create a timeline, putting events in order to explain them later.

Imagine a traumatic event that you can recall as if it was yesterday . . . the picture is so vivid and clear in your mind that you can visualize the overwhelming feelings you felt as if it happened yesterday. Perhaps you have had nightmares or sleepless nights as a result of this event or engage in ritualistic or repetitious behaviors such as chronic hand washing to ease the pain.

When a trauma results in overwhelming pain, anger, shame, and fear become paralyzing. We try to cope with it all kinds of ways but it's like gum stuck on our shoe—we just can't seem to be able to leave it behind us! No one will ever understand the amount of pain and the suffering we are going through and they don't have to. Getting in touch honestly with the feelings that are torturing us is the first step toward putting those feelings behind us.

For those who are suffering from past trauma, I highly recommend finding a specialist who uses Eye Movement Desensitization and Reprocessing (EMDR) and Psych-K(R). EMDR is a comprehensive, integrative psychotherapy approach. It contains elements of many effective psychotherapies in structured protocols that are designed to maximize treatment effects. These include psychodynamic, cognitive behavioral, interpersonal, experiential, and body-centered therapies. Psych-K is a user-friendly way to rewrite the "software" of your mind to change the "printout" of your life. Both of these approaches to treating trauma have shown great results.

Without treatment, it's easy to fall into a powerless, victim-like mind-set, due to self-hatred that is likely to cause you to enter into abusive relationships in which you may sustain more violation and pain. You may even say to yourself, "All I was looking for was love, comfort, and safety . . . how could this happen to me?" At a conscious level, you did look for that love, however, your subconscious was working hard to reinforce your core belief of worthlessness that you are a victim and that the world is about pain and rejection. This is what is familiar as that is how you established your world within you. Sometimes when you least expect it, an isolated event such as a scene from a movie or being trapped in an elevator can trigger very old, yet powerful and debilitating pain. It seems to come out of nowhere. You become frozen, overwhelmed with the surfacing feelings, engulfed in fear as powerful as you experienced when the original trauma occurred. Remembering the trauma and how helpless you were throws you into the grips of natural regression. You become that helpless, wounded child and react in the same manner as you did as a child even though you are an adult. Because you haven't developed the ability to deal with your emotional pain in the present, you will act out your pain by being childish or looking for someone to rescue you.

In some cases, a repeated act such as physical abuse is so painful and overwhelming that the victim may create amnesia as a defense, hindering his ability to recall the event. This prevents recalling the painful memories and feelings or block of time as if they never happened. But no matter what such roadblocks we erect, we are never safe from repressed feelings. Sometimes a simple scent, or image, or sound can trigger the blocked emotion and the walls of denial come crumbling down, leaving us overwhelmed and devastated. Unprepared and confused, self-doubt sinks in and we start questioning our own sanity. Are we imagining this? Or did it really happen? What we distort becomes our reality.

Current Therapy

Joe has been seeing a psychoanalyst for years for treatment of his fear of monsters under his bed. It had been years since he had gotten a good night's sleep. His progress was very poor, and he knew it. One day, he stops seeing the psychoanalyst and decides to try something different. A few weeks later, Joe's former psychoanalyst runs into Joe in the supermarket and is surprised to find him looking well-rested, energetic, and cheerful.

"Doc!" Joe says, "It's amazing! I'm cured!"

"That's great news," the psychoanalyst says. "You seem to be doing much better. How?"

"I went to see another doctor," Joe answers enthusiastically, "and he cured me in just one session!"

"One?!" the psychoanalyst asks incredulously.

"Yeah," continues Joe, "My new doctor is a behaviorist."

"A behaviorist?" the psychoanalyst asks. "How did he cure you in just one session?"

"Oh, easy," says Joe. "He told me to cut the legs off my bed."

One of the reasons why people may not benefit from therapy or achieve the desired outcome has to do with the therapeutic approach. Most of the time people already know what is wrong when they seek therapy. But approaching an emotional problem through logic is a failing proposition. As we've discussed, emotional energy cannot be processed through intellectual energy. Emotional energy must be worked through with primary feelings. Most traditional forms of therapy lead people with deep, unresolved feelings back into the past to uncover the original source of the pain and then come to terms with it. The belief is that the person, now older and wiser and having experienced many years of growth and suffering, will be able to view the old pain with new distance and accuracy and thus be better able to set aside the defenses he has used to deal with that pain. This may be a good theory but does not always work. As we grow up, most of the time we do not gain the perspective on past trauma, pain, or rejection that is necessary to see it more clearly in the present.

Another hurdle is largely due to our belief system, which resides in our subconscious. Talk therapy is primarily a conscious work. Seeking insight and understanding about a past event seldom brings about a resolution because this quest involves communication with the wrong part of the mind. It is like going into a Japanese restaurant where no one speaks your language—you look at the Japanese menu and become even more confused. Although the waiter knows you are hungry and would like to eat, he has no idea what you want. You can detect from his behavior and his facial expressions that he is really trying to help you, but you haven't the faintest idea what he is communicating. As the gestures and the sign language fail, you give up. Until you can find someone who can speak the language, you cannot resolve the problem. The subconscious mind requires a different approach. The language of feelings is conscious as well as subconscious.

Emotional vs. Emotionless

If your life feels empty, it is because you gave nothing to it.
—Casey

When it comes to feelings, there is no difference between men and women; we all feel feelings the same way. In fact, feelings are universal. They are what enable us to understand ourselves and the world we created. Our world is within us; the way we color our world and bring it forth through our feelings creates our reality. Some of us tend to feel many feelings all at once while others are nearly void of feelings.

Emotional

Some of us overcompensate for an inability to get in touch with our real feelings, exaggerating feelings to make our point. In this case, the feelings present as if we are acting a part in a play. It may come as a surprise to learn that those of us who are very emotional people actually have a very difficult time getting in touch with our primary feelings. Often the feelings we present are reactionary feelings, such as self-pity, guilt, and hopelessness. The majority of very emotional people use tears as a way of displaying emotion as if tears are proof of emotional connectedness. But oftentimes we may not even know what we are actually crying about. We may see ourselves as very sensitive and project to the world that we are very fragile. Being emotional allows us to avoid anger, which is a very uncomfortable emotion for many of us. Because we may believe that anger is a bad feeling, the tears and emotional overreaction become our salvation.

Emotionless

Some of us decide very early on to divorce their feelings. In this way, we can avoid any future emotional pain. We live in their own inner world without much understanding of love and intimacy. Being in a relationship with an emotionless person is like having a relationship with your car—don't expect much of anything in return. Emotionless people form better relationships with inanimate objects, such as TVs and computers, because these relationships don't require any intimacy. Those of us who are emotionless have an indifferent reaction to the world. We tend to be loners and pursue jobs that fit that lifestyle. We usually don't feel the need to change, believing that this is as good as it gets or that we are good enough.

Resistance to Change

> *I was thinking about making some changes, I didn't realize my body is already doing it effortlessly.*
> —Casey

Change is difficult, especially if it pertains to our emotional state. Change requires risk-taking; going beyond our comfort zone. Our internal mechanism, driven by our ego, is fearful of how change may affect us, our image, or our feelings. Resistance to change comes in many forms.

Inability to Grasp The Message

In most cases, if a message we are trying to convey is not clear, people are not going to understand where we are coming from. Have you ever been to a foreign country where you asked for help in your native language and received a blank stare in response? If the person you asked doesn't speak your language, they cannot possibly know what you are talking about. In order for change to occur, a message should be easily understood, leaving no room for confusion.

Likability Problem

Getting information from someone we don't like is similar to getting a hug from them. Not good experience. If we already don't care for the person, why should we care about the help or advice they are giving, even though it may have a positive impact in our life? The right message needs to be conveyed by the right person in an acceptable manner. No wonder we are often ready to shoot the messenger and the message due to our contextual feelings toward that person.

Unacceptable subject

When we show interest in something, we are already open to finding out more about it and how it can benefit us. But if the subject matter is something we don't like, that is unacceptable to us, we will be turned off. For example, if we don't like eating liver, yet someone serves it to us along with an explanation of all of the nutritional benefits of eating liver, we are not likely to change our mind. If we don't like it, we don't like it. Period. So it's understandable that those of us who learned not to feel our emotions will react as if we are eating liver—with distaste. In much the same way, if we do not like ourselves, change is particularly difficult.

Defenses—the illusion of self-protection

Defenses, such as denial and intellectualization, are by far the most influential roadblocks in our lives simply because we are our defenses. The primary function of defense is managing pain so that life will not be overwhelming. This serves a valuable purpose, enabling us to survive overwhelming pain such as the loss of a loved one. Unfortunately, many of us have the belief that the world is not a safe place and that our self must be protected at all times firmly established in our psyche. As a result, our walls are up, gloves are on, and we are ready to defend ourselves at any given time.

Defenses—The Illusion of Self-Protection

In medieval times, the threat to the environment was great, so each king built a castle. The thicker and the higher the walls were, the more he was reassured that he was safe. When all was said and done, he felt safe and protected from outside danger. His primary mission was to survive and maintain his castle from which he ruled based upon his fears. But those castle walls also kept the king isolated from the world. In a way, he became the prisoner of the very walls he built to protect himself.

Defense is nothing but a lie that we build to stop our feelings from showing themselves. They are basically a barrier to reality. Everyone has defenses, some of us more that the others. Some of us wear full body armor, while others carry only a shield. Our defenses, like our feelings, become a part of our belief system, regularly activated by our subconscious. When we feel emotionally threatened, our defensive response of anger or fear is not a calculated, conscious response. If our belief system is very distorted (mistaken beliefs) due to toxic emotions, we become much more reactive, always on guard, as if we have a chip on our shoulder. The anger we feel as a result becomes our weapon to deter others from finding out what we are hiding. By deterring others from coming close to us, we manage to mask our shame and character defects with overreaction and anger. The more defended or defensive we are, the more rigid and convoluted we become.

When we live in a defensive world, most of our energy is directed toward keeping our defenses in place. The degree to which we hold on to our defenses will determine how well or to what degree we can process our feelings. If we learned very early on to develop a security system for self-protection, our world became colored by fear. The more we invested in self-protection, the more we lost our emotional self. As we get older we become our defenses. We perceive our defenses as our shelter and strength. In turn, they reinforce the world we created within us. The thicker and the higher our defenses, the more emotionally bankrupt we become. But as we relinquish our need for our defenses, only then are we able to free ourselves from the depths of our emotional prison.

CHAPTER 9 *Relationships*

First the self than the possibility of having a relationship

A relationship can be a place of real personal growth, or it can be a nightmare that stunts our personal growth and/or causes us to relive our past. It is not a coincidence that some of us find ourselves in unfulfilling, difficult relationships without much intimacy; these relationships often resemble our childhood environment and relationship with our parents. Growing up in chaos, conflict, distancing, rejection, or an emotionless environment, the perception of intimacy gets distorted in such a way that intensity assumes the place of intimacy. As a result over time, more emotional baggage gets added to the existing toxic feelings. As the past gets recycled into the present, emotional well-being becomes less and less important as we become fixated on power, right or wrong, blame, etc. When a relationship becomes more like a roller coaster ride, the individuals in the relationship operate more from shame, blame, power, and dominance.

In a "relationship," what we primarily "relate" are feelings. Many couples who seek marital therapy because of a failing relationship will hear from their therapist, "You two have a communication problem" followed by an attempt to teach the couple new communication skills. But I have personally seen many couples who have great communication skills and are able to express themselves well struggle with a deteriorating relationship. This is largely due to the couple's inability to take the risk to express their core feelings. Feelings are the way we communicate with our inner being; it is the only language that works. If we don't understand this language, we cannot expect to communicate with others or form meaningful relationships. Most relationships suffer to some degree but some more than others. Those that struggle the most are formed based upon instant gratifications, such as being lonely, empty, horny, or guilty.

When two people start a new relationship, the sexual and emotional energy are like aphrodisiacs, drawing people together like magnets. Blinded by the physical body's natural opiates, as the couple starts getting more comfortable with each other and establishes a sense of togetherness, they may experience the following relationship pattern:

    1—Assuming roles
    2—Dropping the mask or facade
    3—Establishing a safety zone
    4—Struggle for intimacy or intensity
    5—Disappointment and distancing
    6—Resolution

1-Assuming Roles

A psychiatrist visited a California psychiatric institution and asked a patient, "How did you end up here? What is the nature of your illness?" He got the following reply:

"Well, it all started when I got married. I guess I should never have done it. I married a widow with a grown daughter who then became my stepdaughter. My dad came to visit us, fell in love with my lovely stepdaughter, then married her. So my stepdaughter became my stepmother. Soon my wife had a son who was, of course, my dad's brother-in-law since he is the half-brother of my stepdaughter, who is now, of course, my dad's wife. Since my son is also the brother of my stepmother, he also became my uncle.

And since my wife is my stepmother's mother, that makes her my step-grandmother. Since I am married to my step-grandmother, I am not only my wife's grandson, but also my own grandfather! Now can you understand how I got here?"

After staring blankly at the patient with a dizzy look on his face, the psychiatrist replied, "Move over!"

People who seek healthy relationships have a clear sense of who they are and an ability to express their wants and needs. When in a relationship, they are able to define themselves emotionally, intellectually, and physically while maintaining their autonomy. As they take this gradual journey of getting to know their partner, they go through several relationship stages, such as superficial, companionship, friendship, romantic love. As they progress among stages, they do not assume a role or attempt to redefine themselves. They don't look for that magical soul mate but they strive to be one as they go through the journey.

> *Soul-mates are people who bring out the best in you.*
> *They are not perfect but are always perfect for you.*
> *—Author Unknown*

However, in most relationships, this is not the norm. Assuming roles is the norm and is a very natural process. Because our subconscious mind is in charge, our conscious mind ignores any red flags. The hypnotic feelings of a new relationship cause us to be emotionally numb, and our ability to act upon our gut feelings is diminished. When we don't know who we really are and are feeling emotionally empty, we subconsciously look for someone to complete us. When we find that someone, we see in them our missing perfect self.

For example, if we grow up emotionally lost and feeling insecure, we are likely to seek out someone who is dominant and controlling. What we falsely start out believing is complete and secure may ultimately turn into huge road blocks that stand in the way of intimacy. We may assume the role of a doormat, a codependent, or a victim while our partner becomes a controller or a perpetrator.

An inability to clearly define ourselves and not having a sense of autonomy hinders our ability to establish healthy boundaries.

2-Dropping the mask or facade

> *After we got married he/she changed.*
> —Casey

How often do we hear people make the above statement and tend to agree with it? Change is inevitable over time, but what is the reason for this so-called instant change that occurs shortly after marriage? In reality, no change has taken place, but rather our ego no longer feels the fear of loss or abandonment so we begin to lower our public mask. Most of the time we see glimpses of our partner's true self while dating, but if those glimpses raised any red flags, we ignore them. Falling in love makes us blind and puts us in a state of denial, so we pretend and hope that the warning signs will magically disappear. When our partner's true self emerges more and more frequently after we are married, and our own emotional fog beings to lift leaving us to see more clearly, we become disappointed, confused, and angry with what we see. We start to blame our partner for this "change," but the truth is that the responsibility lies with ourselves. We chose to form this relationship.

3-Establishing a Safety Zone

In healthy relationships, partners are not concerned with safety because the relationship is based on mutual trust and acceptance. Free of fear, as the couple becomes more vulnerable with each other, they grow together while sharing love. But when the couple is emotionally limited, as they arrive to this point in their relationship, each partner tries to determine his own emotional comfort zone. This is once again established based upon how we came to terms with our feelings in early life.

Establishing our comfort level gives us a sense of safety, a comfort zone from which to operate. Functioning beyond this zone becomes difficult as it is scary and unfamiliar. Our subconscious mind likes to work with what is familiar. Even though both we and our partner would like to get much closer, trying to achieve this goal ends in frustration. In the long run, this comfort zone brings boredom and ritualism without much adventure.

4-Intimacy Factor

Every relationship has its ups and downs. What makes a relationship a success is how well both partners are equipped to deal with these challenges to achieve the desired outcome. Partners who establish emotional honesty and strive for intimacy validate each other's feelings and actively take part in solving a conflict. In healthy relationships, joy and comfort is the norm with brief periods of struggle and conflict.

True intimacy is an experiential journey achieved through core feelings. In may relationships couples struggle for intimacy because of their own unexamined shortcomings. When we don't want to admit our emotional limitations to our partner and our subconscious is unwilling to risk exposing our feelings because of fear, we develop defensive patterns instead of feelings. Especially in addictive or abusive relationships, fear is confused with passion and excitement, and thus the concept of an intimate loving relationship is established through this distortion. This is why people who are raised in addictive relationships have a tendency to imitate the love between the addictive parents. In these relationships, pain and struggle, with brief periods of enjoyable moments, is the norm. This is why in these types of relationships intensity is almost always perceived as intimacy. As the relationship evolves, partners slowly start drifting apart while desperately trying to hold it together. The cumulative effect of negative feelings makes each partner more and more resentful, distant, and reactive.

Resentments, which are unresolved feelings, start creating blocks in the intimacy gap like dominoes. As the blocks increase in number, so does the gap between us and our partner. As the relationship gradually turns into battlefield, wrought with arguments, mood swings, drama, and mind games, intimacy gives way to intensity. Because of our inability to be vulnerable, we avoid the truth about ourselves and instead act out our feelings intensely in an attempt to find resolutions. Sometimes, we or our partner hang on to these resentments, not wanting to give them up because they provide a certain edge over the other. Soon we can no longer get past the mounting resentments to truly understand our partner and resolve our difficulties. As the resentments become the main force in the relationship, both we and our partner start drifting apart.

5-Disappointment And Distancing

Healthy relationships thrive on closeness and do not allow room for repeated disappointments. As the unhealthy relationship reaches this stage, we start relying heavily on our defenses, avoiding painful truth, much like we did as children. We make statements such as, "It's not that bad" or "Nothing is wrong" or "I hope things will change." The more defensive we become, the more distant and distorted we feel. The aphrodisiac-like sexual energy seems to slowly give way to guilt and disappointment, reflecting the negative state of our relationships. Feeling desperate and scared, we may offer sex to get love, and yet no amount of sex seems to reassure the failing relationship. Realizing this is a failing proposition, in some cases we turn sex into a very effective weapon of choice, either withholding sex as punishment or demanding it to try to make our partner feeling guilty. At this point, partners are more interested in getting their own needs met through control or manipulation. We lose interest in the relationship and are unwilling to seek professional help, believing that we are the cause of the failed relationship.

7—Resolution

In healthy relationships, conflict resolution is a joint effort in which both partners are committed to resolving the conflict by being actively involved in the process and bringing solutions. Imagine you made a pact with your partner to never go to bed angry. However, in unhealthy relationships, partners will try to solve their conflict by persistent blame, finger-pointing and emotional abuse. Frustration and further alienation become the outcome of their conflict resolution. Ultimately, a decision is made, one way or the other. The direction of that decision depends upon our tolerance for pain and that of our partner. If one of us exceeds our pain threshold, we will choose to separate. However, in abusive relationships (e.g., domestic violence), some partners have the ability to modify their pain tolerance to a state of numbness in which no amount of pain or abuse will drive them to leave the relationship. If neither of us passes our pain threshold, we will choose to stay in the relationship, avoiding our fear of loss or pain by using excuses such as money or kids. We learn to cohabitate in our denial. Because we had hoped to achieve emotional self mastery through these relationships, we cannot escape the bitter truth of our denial and the fact of our emotional bankruptcy.

It is possible for two people to form a relationship devoid of emotional attachment, feeling very comfortable with a superficial, rather than intimate relationship. Consider Jill's story:

I have been married to my husband for about four years. We are both working professionals and do well financially. We do not fight, but when we argue, it is about doing something intimate. After the first six months of marriage, my husband lost interest in sex and emotionally he doesn't share much of anything with me. We have seen a couple of doctors about his sexual problems—they determined that he has low sperm count and sex drive. He did nothing about it. Gradually we came to a place in our marriage where there is no excitement, passion or romance. I feel like I have a roommate, not a husband. Yet it's cozy and very comfortable. But I find myself wondering and fantasizing about other men. I don't think I can continue living like this.

Two years later, I ran into Jill at a grocery store. Looking surprised and bit evasive, she said jokingly, "Well, we are still together. I guess some things are just meant to be." People who form coexisting kind of relationships are usually fearful of getting close to others. They struggle with the idea of rejection or abandonment, although they pretend otherwise, so they settle for less.

Over many years of working with couples, it became evident to me that it is not so much the relationship that needs to be fixed. The relationship is like a playground—what matters isn't the playground itself but what we bring to it. Many of us are ill-equipped, unprepared, and unaware of who we really are. If we enter a relationship as an incomplete person, we are going to end up in an incomplete relationship that will never enable us to feel good about ourselves. When we form a relationship with a wrong person, we create a situation full of stress, erosion of self-esteem, and loss of self-confidence. We start questioning our own judgment and wonder how we got to this point. If we spend our lives looking for the right person and not spending any time looking for ourselves, whatever we find we will surely lose. The person we find to rescue us is never the right person. The person we find to rescue us likely has greater needs than we do.

CHAPTER 10

Coming to Terms With Our Past

There is nothing wrong with our feelings, there is only something wrong with the way we deal with them.
—Casey

A woman notices a drunk man crawling around under a street light on his hands and knees.

"What are you looking for?" the woman asks.

"My car keys," the drunk man responds.

"How did you lose them?" the woman asks.

"They fell out of my pocket in my bedroom," the drunk man answers.

Surprised, the woman asks, "If you lost your keys in your bedroom, why are you looking for them under this street light?"

The drunk man replies, "The light is better here."

Many of us look for solutions in all the wrong places. Our feelings what illuminates dark and they are the source of the answers we seek.

No one is responsible for our feelings but ourselves. If we are hoping for someone to come along and change them for us, we are waiting for a bus that will never come. The journey toward establishing emotional self mastery requires total acceptance of our feelings without any conditions, and how well we learn to process them. We can only attain such wealth when we start telling the truth about our feelings and taking the initiative to direct them to the source without getting in the way.

Some of us create the deception of mistaken beliefs, and hence we feel discomfort with anger; pretending that we are not angry, hoping that the feeling will go away. Some of us feel afraid of our own anger, believing that if we get angry, we may be rejected by others. Some of us don't want to admit to feeling pain, thinking that it makes us look vulnerable, or appear weak to others. Some don't want to admit hurt because, as far as they are concerned, hurt doesn't exist. If we want to achieve inner peace and happiness, we have to leave behind self-deceptions such as these; we have to do the emotional work.

Present Feelings

Your feelings, just like your life, are happening at this moment. The past is a collection of your experiences; the future is a convenient mental construct. We are all promised wealth and happiness in the future—if we work hard enough and be patient enough, it is ours. But when we get there, instead of joy, we find sorrow. Trying to change our past to enrich our lives is like building an igloo in the middle of the desert—a frustrating chore.

To be emotionally free means allowing ourselves to take the steps to express feelings as we experience them in the present. There is no reason for us to hold on to burdensome repressed emotions, knowing the impact and suffering they will cause in our life. However, we need to be present to our feelings as we experience life if we are to confront things as they happen.

Sometimes it's not possible to express our feelings immediately; many circumstances are simply not conducive to this (for example, the middle of a church sermon!). But in these cases, we can decide how and when we will express our feelings, enabling us to come from a place of empowerment and strength and making us less likely to act out or react. In this case, time is our friend as long as the delayed action is for the purpose of taking care of ourselves.

There are two reasons to attend to our feelings in the present:

First, our world is our creation and so are our feelings. We can't escape problems, conflicts, pain, or violation. Instead of putting all our energy into trying to avoid or deny our feelings, we must create the ability and insight to deal with them effectively as they happen. This lets us stop living in the past. Life is happening now; tomorrow may never come. When current feeling is postponed, that feeling often summons other identical unresolved repressed emotions. When these hidden emotions surface, we become overwhelmed and more reactive, confused about which feelings we are responding to. The purpose of processing feelings in the present is to diminish the impact of bottled-up emotions so that our present is not colored with negative feelings from the past. Our ability to take care of ourselves emotionally rewards us with a feeling of enlightenment. No longer will we carry the world on our shoulders. No longer will we live in a state of projected anxiety as we have more to love and less to fear. As we learn to trust our gut feelings instead of making them our enemy, we become more intuitive and able to reach a level of higher consciousness. Self-love is the act of being aware and giving ourselves the gift of being present in our feelings.

Second, when our energy flows freely, we are free—free of our past and the worries about our future. When we no longer repress our feelings, our emotional energy has the ability to connect with our spiritual energy, thereby achieving higher wisdom. Since we no longer fight with ourselves, our positive energy is channeled inward, enabling us to experience our inner world and to reconnect with our god, our higher power, our true purpose.

> *A troubled mind will thunder*
> *A troubled heart will suffer*
> *But if you reach deep within,*
> *Your spirit will greet you with wonder.*
> —Casey

Processing Old Resentments

> *It's not because you are hung up on the past—your unresolved emotions won't let you be free.*
> —Casey

Why We Resent

Resentments are a major force when it comes to how much emotional wealth we can achieve. Resentments are those negative emotions that have the power to enslave us to the past. Sometimes it is possible to harbor deep resentments and not be aware of the hold they have on us. Even though we know that resentments do not serve us in a good way, we still allow them to accumulate. Some of us even achieve this false notion that holding on to resentments keeps us at a distance, and thus safe from those who hurt us. When our ego gets bruised by pain, a strong ego defense in the form of resentments assures self-preservation. However, in the long run, we inevitably hurt ourselves the most. All resentment is withheld feelings with which we are unwilling to come to terms. We are often encouraged to let go, yet this is easier said than done—many of us do not know what to let go of or how to do it. If we are holding on to a rope and no longer want to pull because we are exhausted, we will let go of the rope to free ourselves. Emotionally, the process is the same. We need to recognize the rope (resentment), identify the emotional makeup, and then release it to the source and let go.

Whether the feelings are toxic, old, or new, they all have to be processed in the present because what we felt in the past and what we feel in the present are very much alike. Once again, if we can't identify with our feelings, it doesn't really matter when and why they occurred.

Resentments Toward Parents

> *As we grow older we end up become like one of our parents and marrying the other.*
> —Casey

When we deal with resentments toward our parents, we may find ourselves struggling. It is difficult to admit that by protecting our parents, we protect our own feelings, and that as a result, we become an extension of those feelings.

In most cases, we become the parent we most resent, although in some cases we become entirely the opposite of that parent. As we grow and become a parent ourselves, we may realize that some of our parents' negative qualities, or our unresolved issues with them, are very much a part of our life. Although we may try very hard not to let these issues influence our relationship with our own children, sometimes they surface when we least expect it, and we end up doing the very thing to our children that we resented our parents doing to us. Having children provides us the opportunity to grow in the relationship between ourselves and our children the way we wanted to grow in a relationship with our parents. Being a parent is not only a privilege, it is a second chance to grow in the way we need to grow. If we are unable to grow, we will be lonely forever, looking for other people to give us what we have to give to ourselves. We have the choice to either live a life of secrets or resentments or to come to terms with our resentments and grow beyond our parents, who may not have been capable of giving us what we need, by being a better parent ourselves.

Identify Your Resentments

Write down all of your resentments, making sure that they are specific. Write by hand instead of using a computer as writing enables you to connect better. After each resentment, stop and simply feel what feelings come up, then write down those feelings next to the resentment. For example, "I resented when you did not show up for my high school graduation. I feel sad, hurt, and angry." Continue to do this until you cannot think of any new resentments.

Process your resentment with your parent

Dos

- Make sure you are emotionally ready to face your parent.

- Make sure you are isolated in a safe place with your parent.

- Make sure you keep an eye contact when you express your feelings.

- Allow yourself to feel—if you cry or get angry, you are being natural.

- Remember when you express your feelings honestly, you will get the power you didn't have when you were a child. Empowering is healing.

- When you are done, thank your parent for listening to you.

- Last, when you are alone, tear up or burn the resentments, letting the grief come to a closure.

Don'ts

- Don't try to present your resentments if you are not emotionally up to it. If you are coming from a place of self-doubt, fear, or confusion, this process will not serve you and will make you feel even worse.

- Don't worry about your parent's feelings. You are not doing this to take care of him or her. You are merely taking care of your old business.

- Don't regress and become that wounded child. If your parent cries, don't interfere.

- If your parent insists the other parent needs to be present also, stay firm and say no. This is a manipulative attempt to deter you from your mission.

- If your parent gets angry or leaves the room, continue reading until you are done with your resentments. You already have your answer. It is time to move on.

- At the end of the process, if your parent makes a statement such as, "None of that ever happened" or "You are crazy" or "You are brainwashed," don't waste your time trying to convince him otherwise. Remember you process your resentments for you to release those trapped, toxic feelings. This process is to enrich your emotional life.

- Expect nothing but your own personal empowerment, otherwise you set yourself up for disappointment.

This process is not about achieving any desired outcome or expectations that your parents will change for you. It is about growing beyond your parents so that you can be better parent yourself. Your parent(s) may have been in and out of your life for various reasons, and this process reconnects you with them after many years. Whether you felt abandoned or rejected or abused by them, those feelings will come alive. Understand that they are who they are. If you decide to process your resentments within a therapy session, more likely your parent will treat you in the same manner he or she has in the past. There is no need to set yourself up for more abuse. So bring your parent to therapy only to take care of yourself. If your parents are not alive, processing your resentments at their grave site is a very cleansing experience. After you finish reading your resentments, just tear up the paper, throw it down, and walk away with a glow in your heart. Whether you are traumatized or abused, or were not loved by your parents, you must let go of your past, put it behind you and allow it to fade.

Take hold of and build the future so that you are free to be the inner energy that has always been within you. It has been there your whole life, it will be there when you leave this life, and you will take it with you. But you must free that energy for it to manifest itself. When you do so, you will be naturally happy and content. All you need to do is heed the bidding of your inner self, see the obstacles to that goal as mere representations of your weaker self, and step around them. Stop hating people, objects, and things because you are afraid of looking at yourself.

Resentments In The Relationship

Resentments are more of a symptom rather than the problem. The real problem lies with the people who are participating in the relationship. If we are becoming gradually more resentful of our partner, this is a clear indicator that our relationship is strained; the road is blocked and the relationship is in danger. No amount of hoping or wishing will change the situation for the better—they will only make it worse. If we are unable to get in touch with our feelings and be honest about our hurt, our relationship is doom to fail or become an endless roller coaster ride. Our unwillingness to find out what we have in our relationship stops us from taking the risk to find out the real truth. Expressing our resentments is our truth and our anchor in our relationships. The power of that expression sets us free.

How to Process Relationship Resentment

- Write down your specific resentments.

- Choose a time where you and your partner are alone without the kids, cell phones and TV turned off.

- Tell your partner your resentments without rushing, making sure that you are in touch with your feelings.

- When you are finished, ask your partner what he/she is feeling and then ask what feelings he/she heard.

- If you believe your partner was attentive and you were able to release your feelings out, express appreciation to your partner for listening, get a hug, tear up the paper and get rid of it.

- Encourage your partner to process his or her resentments at another time. This should focus on your partner's true resentments, however, not a retaliation or justifications for your resentments.

Use this process as often as possible as the need arises to keep both you and your partner free from negative feelings. Resentment robs us of our positive creative energy and hinders our spiritual journey. Our ability to deal with our feelings as we experience them allows us to conquer our resentments. This is the best gift we can give ourselves. When we are no longer harboring negative emotions, we are free to grow and free to love.

Forgiveness

Turn the other cheek but
My other cheek is already black and blue.
—Casey

Forgiveness is one of the most misunderstood concepts. We are taught to believe that we must forgive those who hurt us to start our own healing. This is easier said than done. First of all, this concept is very flawed as it asks us to turn the other cheek when someone hurts us. This is very misleading and may even expose us to further self-violation and pain. Life without pain does not exist; along the way we are intentionally or unintentionally hurt by others. By simply saying "I forgive you," we are trying to come to terms with our pain through our conscious mind, while our emotional and spiritual bodies believe otherwise. Some of us may be convinced that we can simply forgive somebody as easily as this, not understanding that we still experience the painful conflict deep within. No matter how many times we say to ourselves that we have forgiven someone, we can't fool our spiritual body. Forgiveness is possible when we come from love and honesty and are able to let go of pain.

There are two important factors we must take into consideration before we commit ourselves to the process of true forgiveness:

Intent

It is unfortunate that we get hurt, but what was the motivation of the person who hurt us? This we may never know. Some acts of pain can be unintentional yet still cause lifelong consequences. A single act of violation can be confusing and hard to understand, but any repeated act or behavior clearly conveys an intent to hurt us. Such violating behaviors clearly display the perpetrator's worldview, which is that they must violate others to fulfilling their own needs. Although the perpetrator may deny, lie or try to manipulate us into thinking this is not the case, we must not doubt ourselves. It is the intent behind that act that causes the most pain. We must simply accept the fact that there are some toxic people in this world, and toxic they will stay. Confronting or forgiving these people is an exercise in futility as their core being is centered around intent to harm others. It is best to simply accept who they are and bid them good riddance.

Pretense

One of the worst things we can put ourselves through after being violated by a family member is to try to pretend that everything is just fine. We may try to convince ourselves that we forgave that family member and try to act as if nothing ever happened when we are around them. Our outward expression is one of happy while our heart is ripped to pieces subconsciously each time we are in the person's presence. When we assume such a pretentious role, we are simply opening ourselves up for further pain and injury, even though the family member may not be doing anything harmful at this time. When we are children, we are unable to protect ourselves, and thus felt like a victim, but our willingness to pretend in the face of pain as an adult makes us a volunteer for further harm. Forgiveness is not pretending to be family or friends with those who have hurt us.

Forgiveness is the process of forgiving the very self as we grieve the pain of an incident out of our emotional body, finally coming to terms with it by letting it go. It has nothing to do with forgiving the person who caused the pain. Remember, most of our problems stem not from the person who caused the pain but from how we reacted to it. When our emotional and spiritual bodies work in tandem without distorting the truth, healing begins naturally. No matter what wrongs were done to us, none can compare to the damage we do to ourselves by believing we are doomed or a victim.

CHAPTER 11 — *Belief Factor*

The belief that becomes truth for me
Is that which allows me to best use my strength
Best means of putting my virtues in action.
—Andre G.

We are ultimately responsible for creating our own emotional wealth, just as we are ultimately responsible for creating our own reality, our own thoughts and emotion, and our own beliefs. Many of us believe that life simply happens to us, but in fact we are the architects of our own reality. To grasp this idea requires a higher level of consciousness. Until we achieve this higher level, we will remain stuck where we are with limited ability to grow beyond our current state.

We perceive our world through our five senses—sight, smell, taste, touch, and hearing. Through these senses we create our perceptions. Our beliefs and our emotions are primarily how we react to these perceptions. This is important because feelings define our perceptions and eventually form various types of beliefs. Some beliefs are strong, some are confusing, and some are mistaken. But whatever we experience early in life through our senses shapes our emotional reactions in the future. Beliefs cause some individuals to be heroes while others live life as defeatists. Our beliefs can literally create or destroy—their power is unlimited. We each have the ability to make positive changes in our lives, yet we tend to be held back at a subconscious level by fear-based beliefs. Not understanding our subconscious beliefs, we repeatedly sabotage any effort toward personal growth. Unless we recognize our toxic mistaken beliefs and change them, our journey to emotional self mastery is unattainable. Earlier we looked at how our emotional, physical and spiritual bodies worked together. As we start forming our belief system, those beliefs impact each of these three centers of our being.

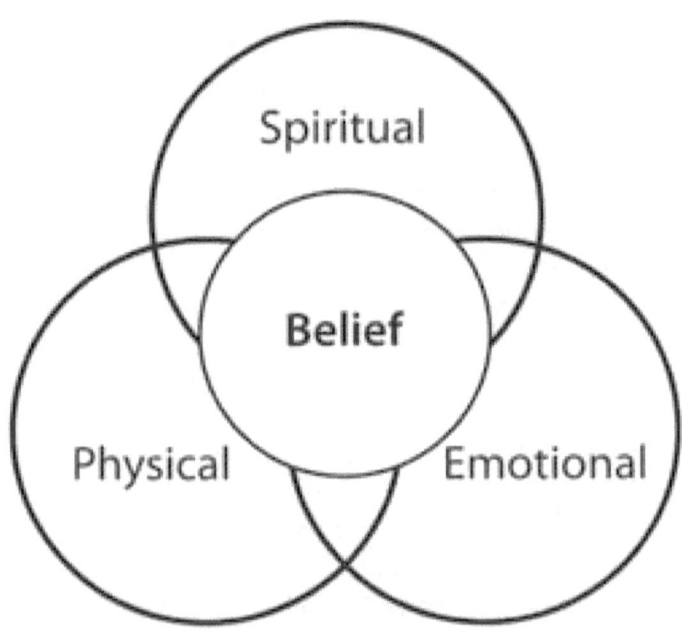

Our mistaken beliefs become a dominating factor in our life because we perceive them as real, and they impact how we respond to the world. This toxic belief system taints every aspect of our being as we create a reality that not only reflects these beliefs, but also our emotions, thoughts, and behaviors are regulated and modified to reflect our belief system.

Let's say you believe you are fat. This belief manifests in your physical body through your hatred of your body parts and distorted perceptions. Your emotional body responds with anger and self-hatred, which may surface as acting out in the form of binge and purge cycles. Your spiritual body responds in shame and self-abuse because it can't relate to self-love. In this way, your belief system profoundly affects your mental health, your physical health, and your spiritual outlook.

What Are Beliefs?

> *It's the mind that makes it good of ill*
> *That makes it rich of happy, rich or poor.*
> —Edmund Spencer

Beliefs are conclusions derived from information and/or experience. Beliefs can be both conscious and subconscious. Our initial sensory experience and how it is interpreted for us is reinforced by our developing nervous system. The nervous system develops as a response to sensory stimuli that creates a certain perception of the world. That perception of the world then structures our belief system.

How Do We Create Our Belief System?

Perception is our awareness shaped and controlled by our beliefs. To create a belief, we have to rely on information. For example, most of us are told that when people die, they go to heaven. We are shown a picture of heaven with angels and saints. Based upon this information, we form the belief that when people die they go to heaven. The other way of creating a belief is through experience. For example, one day, my friend, his two-year-old son and I went to the grocery store. While we were busy debating an issue and not paying attention, his son climbed out of the shopping cart and fell to the ground, hitting his head really hard. The pain, without a doubt, was excruciating. A month later, the three of us happened to go to the grocery store again. As we walked in and my friend grabbed a shopping cart, his son ran to me and grabbed on to my leg. Based upon the child's painful previous experience with a shopping cart, his reaction to this shopping cart was directed by fear. This perception of fear establishes how to avoid future pain, which becomes his reality, and thus "shopping carts are dangerous" becomes his belief. This ultimately affects future perception. There are several factors that influence belief formation in your subconscious mind—your relationship with your parents, your environment, your childhood experiences, and social conditioning.

Cycle of Negative Belief Formation

Almost all of our beliefs come from someone else's desire for control or their need to be right. Negative belief systems are formed innocently, yet we believe that those are the truths about how we see our world. Our belief system rarely reflects our personal truth. We first have to release our negative belief system to find out what is true for each of us. The following diagram is an example of how those negative beliefs are created and reinforced:

CYCLE OF NEGATIVE BELIEF FORMATION

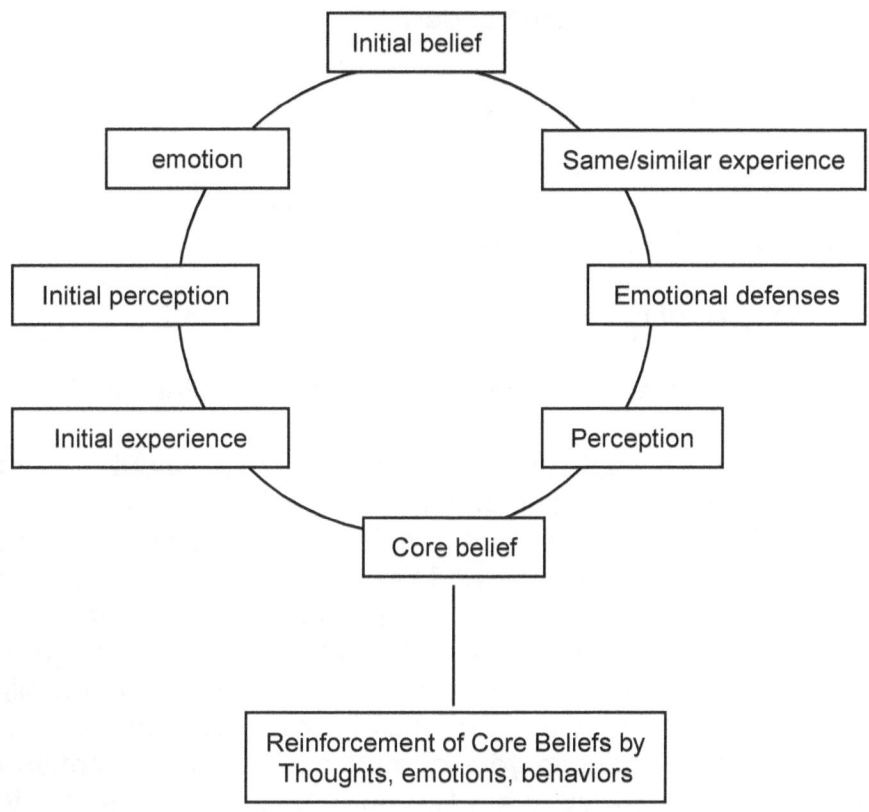

As negative beliefs are regularly reinforced, they don't feel negative; they feel normal. Our subconscious mind is already programmed in these negative belief cycles just like the hard drive of a computer. We can only access what is in there, not what we think we should have. The power of negative beliefs cannot be ignored. Some examples of negative beliefs include, "I'm worthless," "I'm unlovable," "I don't trust myself," "I'm a failure," "I can't trust people," and "I am so stupid."

What are your negative beliefs? Write them down. You may be amazed at what you have been harboring without realizing it. Then consider the following questions in relation to each belief statement:

- How did the belief come about?

- Why do I believe it?

- How did I create that?

- How would I feel if I stopped believing that?

- Is fear part of my belief?

- Does this belief serve me or someone/something else?

Most often we do not run around telling others about our core beliefs, we just simply think and act on them as they are our truth and our perceived reality. For example, you may accidentally lock your keys inside of your car and find yourself saying something like, "I can't believe I did this! I'm so stupid!" At the time, your self-judgment seems appropriate, and your intellect can justify that kind of a statement. However, what you likely do not realize is that this event met a subconscious need to reinforce your shame belief to maintain your current reality and perception of who you are. This may seem like an innocent process, but the consequences of this kind of self-reinforcement are lifelong.

Emotional Beliefs

Dealing with deep-rooted emotional beliefs is not as easy as some of us may think. A belief that is formed out of information is much easier to face than a belief that is based around strong negative emotions. An event in the present may evoke something vaguely familiar in the past and may even identify with an accompanying emotion at the same time. However, sometimes the present event may bring up a very painful past trauma along with overwhelming feelings. When we experience a single traumatizing event as a child, the negative emotions attached to that event may or may not lead to a belief formation. The extent of the trauma, the intensity of that negative emotion, and the other negative emotions that may also attach to this event determine the outcome of belief formation. The more traumatizing the experience, the more likely it will be the dominant reference point, or emotional belief from which we react when we experiences similar events in the present. Also, because of these emotionally charged beliefs, it's more likely that we will over identify with one hemisphere of the brain when the trauma is recalled.

Fred lost both of his parents in a car accident at the age of seven. Every time Fred saw a car accident, he was immediately reminded of the pain of losing his parents. At the same time, his subconscious mind was able to reinforce his belief system, which said, "Don't get close to anyone, you may lose them too."

The cumulative effect of trauma that is repeated, such as ongoing physical abuse, creates dominant beliefs. These dominant beliefs become the point of reference for any similar emotions in the present. Multiple repeated events attach to the subconscious like the fish hooks, very hard to remove. Although an abused child attempts to shield himself from most of the negative emotions by denying them, he cannot stop them from forming the core beliefs that shape his world. Because these core beliefs carry very highly charged emotions, they will always take the center stage when a similar emotion is experienced in the present. This is why when we recall these negative emotions, because of their cumulative effect, we become highly exaggerated and intense. The belief becomes strongly anchored. As we try to deal with an event from the past, we may become overwhelmed and disappointed because we don't experience the expected relief, and in fact may feel much worse. In talk therapy, this may become very evident. Since the subconscious beliefs are difficult to work through using a conscious process as we attempt to heal ourselves, the anchored belief merely causes us to recycle our painful emotions without any release. The inability to differentiate the current emotions from those of highly charged old emotions keeps us living in the past without realizing it. We ultimately believe that the world is a cruel, painful place, and any present emotions not only reinforce our core beliefs but also reassure us that we are right. Hence, these beliefs are coded in our subconscious for the rest of our lives while creating spontaneous points of reference. These core beliefs play a major factor in how we perceive ourselves. As we become an adult, we may reenact past beliefs by assuming a role such as being a rager and violating others repeatedly or being a perpetual victim looking to be rescued.

Brain vs. Mind

> *Is the human brain, at some primal level a*
> *Wonderful computer linked with a*
> *Universal energy field, that knows*
> *Far more that it knows it knows?*
>
> —E. Whalen

The brain is primarily a vast electrical system. The wiring of the system is driven by two forces—genetics, and more importantly, experiences. Considering we now know that the wiring of a child's brain is largely determined by events experienced well into adolescence, we can begin to understand how important it is for us to foster experiences that are positive instead of negative. That's what makes the parenting job so important.

The brain is made out of two hemispheres: the right brain and the left brain. A great deal of research has been conducted for decades on what is called "brain dominance theory." Research findings clearly indicate that each hemisphere of the brain tends to specialize in and preside over different functions.

The Right Brain

The right brain processes information in parallel. It is all about this moment, thinks in pictures, and learns kinesthetically through the movement of our bodies. It is characterized as female. Information in the form of energy streams into the body through all of our sensory systems and then is interpreted. The right brain uses intuition and emotions. It is how we connect to one another. It identifies with the group.

The Left Brain

The left brain thinks in words. It thinks sequentially and methodically about the past and future. It takes in information, in all of its detail, then categorizes and organizes it, associating it with everything in the past we ever learned and projecting it into future possibilities. It is characterized as male. The left brain is an ongoing brain chatter that connects our internal world to our external world. It's that calculating intelligence that reminds us of everything. It identifies with the individual.

Why is this information pertinent? Although we have a natural ability to simultaneously activate both parts of our brain, our life experiences create dominance of one side over the other when responding to specific situation. As the mind over identifies with either side, it can contribute to massive conflicts since it becomes the major driving force. The goal is to increase the ability of both hemispheres to communicate with each other effectively in order to achieve whole brain function. This is very helpful in changing the toxic beliefs that lurk in our subconscious and in reaching our full potential.

Conscious Mind vs. Subconscious Mind

Reality is merely an illusion, albeit a persistent one.
—A. Einstein

Remember the first time you tried to learn how to ride a bicycle? You tried to get on the bicycle, tried to balance yourself, screaming at times, repeatedly falling, occasionally getting hurt, while your conscious mind was actively involved in this first experience. After a while you became an expert. Not only were you riding well, you were able to do many tricks. Even if you didn't ride your bicycle for a long time, when you got back on it you could ride with no problem as if you had never taken a break. But what if every time you got on your bike it was as difficult as the first time? What a chore that would be! We can thank our subconscious mind for saving us from this arduous experience by recording everything for us so that we don't have to relearn it. This programming applies to most everything from early childhood, including our beliefs, emotions, experiences, behaviors, and thoughts. The working of the two minds is truly magical.

Let's explore the two minds and their functions

The conscious mind

- Time-bound; past and future

- Volitional; sets goals and judges, tries new things

- Thinks abstractly; thinks great ideas

- Short-term memory; average length is about twenty seconds

- Limited processing capacity; one to three events, averages 2,000 bits of information per second

The subconscious mind

- Timeless; communicates in the present time

- Habitual; monitors operations of the body; prefers what is familiar

- Thinks literally; sees the world through the five senses

- Long-term memory; stores past experiences, memories

- Expanded processing capacity; thousands of events; averages 4 billion bits of information per second

Unfortunately, when negative beliefs are programmed in our subconscious, we primarily respond to our present based upon what is in there, our so-called "old tapes." Remember, it is our subconscious mind that stores our long-term memory, our past experiences, the emotions that are attached to those experiences and behaviors. Yet we persist in trying to use our conscious mind to resolve past issues. It's like needing money, and instead of going to the bank to get cash, we go to a blood bank not understanding why we are there and why we can't resolve our problem. Engaging the subconscious mind in a battle with our conscious mind is no different—it's an exercise in futility.

According to Emmanuel Donchin, director of the laboratory for Cognitive Psychophysiology at the University of Illinois, as much as 99 percent of cognitive activity may be nonconscious.[41] So as adults, instead of consciously creating our life, we spend most of our time subconsciously responding to it. It should be clear by this point that trying to change our habitual behaviors, toxic beliefs, toxic emotions, and behaviors through reasoning is a waste of time and a recipe for failure. This is why all the positive thinking, self-affirmations, and motivational seminars do not have any impact—they do not directly communicate with the subconscious.

Our free will is the extension of our conscious mind, meaning that we are able to make decisions that we are not totally helpless. This means we have to be conscious every moment of our lives and rely on our will power. For instance, when we are driving and find that we have no idea how we got from point A to point B, we get startled and scared. This demonstrates that when conscious mind is not paying attention, the subconscious programs take over. This also explains why most addicts repeatedly relapse even though consciously they are working very hard to stay sober. When the toxic belief of "shame" becomes part of our subconscious programming, no amount of will power or trying harder will override it.

---

[4] Brain/Mind Collections. March 5, 1984. Vol. 9. No. 6A.

Shame And Toxic Shame

We experience feeling ashamed when our personal values are violated by our behavior. We think, "I did something I know I am not supposed to do. I made a mistake. I feel ashamed." Toxic shame is an inner sense of being unworthy, inadequate, bad, and insufficient as a person. It is an identity wherein the self-judges the self. Shame is like a fine mist; we cannot see it, and yet gradually we get soaked. "I feel ashamed" is a feeling, while "I am shamed" is a belief.

Those of us who are shame-based believe that we deserve to be punished. This belief makes us feel responsible for everything that goes wrong in our life. As shame gradually erodes our self, our internal response results in the loss of self-worth and self-confidence, ultimately leaving us feeling worthless. "I feel unlovable" and "I can never measure up" become our core beliefs, the source of our shame.

Toxic shame has more to do with our childhood and the emotional injuries we sustained in the family system. Shame is about secrets that we learn to carry throughout our life because of an unspoken agreement with our parents to stay loyal to their emotional dishonesty no matter what. The ways in which our family encouraged us to misrepresent the truth becomes part of our toxic shame and mistaken belief. Until we recognize and admit the feelings that silenced us, we will continue to support the family shame. We may love our family and still care deeply for those who violated us, but until we recognize the emotional need to protect them and how our secrecy corrupted our core being, we are not any different than our parents.

Shame is regularly reactivated in order to maintain its place in the system. Consequently, many of us struggle with the idea of self-worth or deservability. Since being deserving is very much tied in with being able to receive, to be happy, to live in peace, and to experience self-love, the application of being deserving in this shame-based system becomes a self-defeating act (or futile experience).

Mike and his wife seemed to benefit from their first six months of therapy; they were able to communicate and resolve issues without acting out for the first time in many years, thus providing harmony and peace. Mike got two promotions, worked out at a health spa, and lost fifty-seven pounds. But one day after work, he discovered his new car had been vandalized. He became enraged. Out of control, he went home and exploded at his wife. Two hours later, he was arrested for beating his wife. Although Mike knew well the consequences of acting out, it was inevitable that his powerful rage would eventually overcome his reason. In six short months of therapy, he never got around to addressing the underlying cause of his low sense of self-worth, his shame.

Shame is protected each time it's acted out, sabotaging recovery just when everything seems to be going well. After all, relapse is a shaming end to an undeserving happy cycle.

Shame is probably the most difficult emotion to face as it evokes frustration and helplessness. Too often, we cling to a false sense of safety rather than taking the risk to discover what is beyond our shame. Shamed people are like flashers in that both hide themselves from the outside world. But unlike flashers who ultimately expose themselves, shamed people believe that they are not good or lovable, and so they hide their true selves. When shamed people inadvertently drop their guard, they feel naked or exposed, and experience shame all over again. Many people believe keeping these personal or family secrets is an act of privacy. Others believe it makes them mysterious. What they don't realize is that their sworn secrecy protects the shame for yet another generation. Only by working through our feelings can we understand and come to terms with toxic shame. Working on shame requires patience, resilience, and love.

Facing ourselves is a difficult and painful process of layer-by-layer revelation and yet at the same time, a very freeing act. Just as in the peeling of an onion, each layer is harder, more uncomfortable, and depending on the toxicity of the impending pain, able to make us cry. Shame is the core of the onion.

Steps to Eliminating Shame

Healing our mistaken core beliefs and toxic shame is the gateway to spirituality. Once we are willing to take responsibility for our feelings, we must start unveiling the iceberg we have been hiding. Why open that can of worms? Because when we take the risk of looking at ourselves and the damage we have created, there is growth. Many of us are forever repeating our past, getting stuck in the same old cycle. It is not our past but those unresolved feelings that won't let us be free.

Step 1: Acknowledge Your Shame

It is difficult sometimes to admit that shame exists. We may feel that our mom and dad did the best they could. We may feel that our upbringing was perfectly normal because we have nothing with which to compare it. Answer truthfully: Were you emotionally and/or physically deprived? Were you neglected? Were your boundaries violated?

Step 2: Identify Your Shame

If you have admitted that shame exists, you need to identify what it is. You may have experienced more than one shaming event in which case you must deal with each separately.

Step 3: Maintain Your Shame

Describe the ways you set yourself up to be shamed. What behavior or situations do you take part in to maintain your toxic shame? Are you aware of this behavior?

Step 4: Get to The Root Of Your Shame

As you start taking this journey into your past, write down the shaming events and perpetrators to the best of your ability. You may not recall the events and the situations exactly. Accept what you remember or what is surfacing without prejudice and blame. Accept the struggle as some of these painful events were denied in early years for your survival and may not be exactly the same. Remember you are not taking a test. Just take ownership of these emotions without self-doubt. You are not crazy; it is those emotions that make you feel that way.

Step 5: Externalize Your Shame

Ultimately, we are responsible for what has happened to us and the kind of shame we have experienced. We may have been molested or abandoned as a child. Maybe we had no choice at the time, but how we came to terms with each painful event was clearly our decision. Take a look at the events, write down the emotions you felt at the time, and note how you feel now. You may find the feelings you have now are those you should have felt in the past. For example, when Jack looked at how he was molested as a child by his uncle, he felt fear and paralysis. But when he read his shame letter during a group counseling session, he felt overwhelming pain, shame, and rage. As you face your shame with your feelings, allow yourself to depart from a state of being and move into a state of feelings.

Step 6: Shrink your shame

Think of your shame as an apple and start taking bites out of it. Shame reduction comes from confronting those who shamed you and expressing your feelings. Writing your resentments and expressing them face-to-face will (as explained earlier) give you the inner strength to detach yourself from the shame and to open the door for establishing your true inner being.

Step 7: Grieve Of your Shame

It is very painful to admit that we were robbed of part or all of our childhood years. We must grieve for that lost childhood. The length of grieving is largely determined by the level of toxicity and our willingness to work on it. However, it is a mistake to think it is a lifelong process. This view simply adds to our prolonged helplessness and victim-like position. A support or therapy group helps process the shame faster and easier.

Step 8: Shame Resolution, Whole Brain Process

Remember, conscious work is limiting when it comes to dealing with subconscious toxic beliefs. This is where the whole brain integration Psych-K work comes in. It's simple, effective, and produces verifiable outcome. More on this topic shortly.

Change your beliefs, change your world

Socrates was on trial for encouraging his students to challenge the existing beliefs of the time and think for themselves. At his trial for heresy, Socrates said, "The unexamined life is not worth living" and his sentence was death. He had the option of suggesting either life in prison or exile in order to avoid his death. He believed that these alternatives did not provide the possibility of "examined life" so he decided there was no point in living.

As we've discussed, pursuing the cause and the source of a problem in therapy does not result in changing beliefs because this approach does not communicate with the subconscious mind. Gaining insight seldom produces lasting changes. Trying to increase willpower also falls short. The following is a great example:

George is a practicing attorney and a sex addict. George has been battling with his sex addictions for many years, and yet none of his family members were aware of the extent to which he was suffering. George regularly visited certain massage parlors soliciting for sex. He got arrested during a sting operation during which he paid an undercover police officer money for sex. He was put on probation and agreed to seek help and do some community work. When he came to my office, he was paranoid that everyone in his law firm knew what happened, but his biggest fear by far was that his wife would find out what happened. He knew well the negative consequences of what could happen to him. After he finished the required number of therapy sessions, he did not want to continue; he felt he had learned his lesson. Four months later he was rearrested for trying to pick up a prostitute. George was in total disbelief when he returned to therapy, not understanding how could this have happened to someone as smart as him, knowing full well what the consequences were going to be. His total lack of understanding of the self-destructive nature of his belief created the outcome. As he relied heavily on his intellect and conscious mind for salvation, he disregarded the true nature of his real problem, his subconscious beliefs.

Earlier, we covered the impact of being emotionally lost and how having incorporated these toxic beliefs into our lost emotional self seems insurmountable to overcome. For many years, we have mastered our illusions as reality and lived in a world of distortions, not realizing why we still suffer. But as we have learned earlier, we can master our emotions and our false beliefs by tapping into our subconscious and speaking its language.

The best way to tap into our subconscious is through muscle testing. Muscle testing, or kinesthetic testing, has been practiced since 1940. It has been used by chiropractors as applied kinesiology to discover physical imbalances. But because our subconscious mind regulates motor functions in the body, including muscle movements, muscle testing also provides a way to communicate with our subconscious.

Psych-K

> *You are not stupid you just can't seem to be able to stop repeating stupid things.*
> —Casey

But the fact is you can. My many years of teaching people how to master their emotions and seeing the amazing results have made me humble. However, for some the struggle was long and arduous. I was very aware of the power and the influence of people's beliefs and the role they played in their self-healing. I have treated very intelligent people who were aware of both the nature of their problems as well as the lifelong consequences they were facing, such as the potential loss of a partner, license, business, and family, yet they continued to self-destruct. Over the years, it became clear to me that self-sabotaging acts are already built in to one's belief system. Daily affirmations, will power, and insight are simply not enough to stop the inevitable downward spiral. When we put belief and thought into action simultaneously, belief almost always wins. People will sometimes even die over what they believe even though it may not be reasonable.

When I discovered Psych-K, I realized that, finally, I can put the pieces together for a more comprehensive approach to self-transformation that really works. Psych-K was created and developed by Robert Williams. The process uses muscle testing to communicate with the subconscious beliefs and employs various methods to eliminate them. As we have discussed, conscious communications is of no use to the subconscious. The subconscious thinks literally, using its own sensory-based language. The statement "I want to be happy," is an abstract statement, which is difficult for the subconscious mind to comprehend and to process. Earlier, we discussed how our subconscious mind is sensory based, thus our communication with our subconscious can only be achieved through sensory-based language. So to communicate "happy" to our subconscious, we have to describe it in terms such as what happy looks like and what happy sounds like.

Psych-K is a unique process that teaches us to get in touch with our mistaken beliefs and facilitate changes. This is a very powerful process that relies on our inner wisdom and ability to make the necessary changes. Psych-K does not promote powerlessness, lifelong process or lifelong grieving. Instead, Psych-K gives us the ability to empower ourselves to make desired changes in our core being.

Is there a light at the end of the tunnel?

*Along with the philosophers reduction of
All objective reality to a shadow world of
Perceptions, scientist have become aware of the
Alarming limitations of the men's senses.*
—Lincoln Barnett

From the beginning, we are conditioned into believing that the world we live in is an absolute material reality. We grow up with this belief and build our entire life around this illusion. This is one of the main reasons why many people are physical-body dominant. Reinforcing this belief with our senses puts our emotional and spiritual bodies at a disadvantage, hence these two bodies receive very little attention and understanding throughout our adult lives. The information we know about our external world is conveyed to us by our five senses. When we are awake, we talk to people, travel, have sex, have scary moments, and so on. When we are dreaming, we also seem to be able to talk to people, travel, have sex, have scary moments, and so on. Yet when we wake up, we realize that our body has not moved; we have only traveled in our subconscious mind. But now you are ready to take a trip in your conscious mind.

The reason we consider our dreams to be not real and the world to be real is nothing but a product of our prejudices. Which one is real is a deception caused by our beliefs and self-conditioning. As long as we measure life through our senses, we will never know our true nature, the nature of reality, or the purpose of life. This is a very narrow existence. We become separated, isolated, and distorted. Earlier, we talked about the desire that emanates from our spiritual body and how we end up fulfilling those desires on the physical plane. Now that we know we have mastered this narrow, materialistic existence, unless our desire to master the ability to connect with the greater, nonphysical reality is greater, we will never experience this higher source, power, god as we will come to know.

We are like a radio tuned in to a certain station with a certain frequency. We are able to receive these energy frequencies and turn them in to sounds and music. We are happy as we perceive that this is all that is possible. The day we choose not to seek the possible existence of other stations and the source that makes this all possible, we have missed our chance to know our highest self. When we finally seek to know God or our higher power, only then will we be rewarded with the experiential knowledge of supreme love. The only difference between those privileged few who have experienced this supreme love and those who have not is that those who have not are not open to experience it. And when we do, then we will know for sure where we came from, what we are, and where we are going. Just as when we wake from a dream, one day we can wake to the true reality of life on earth.

Someone once asked me, "If I came here because of a loving God, then why is God so unkind and I have been suffering?" We were all in the presence of God's body until we decided to be in human body. We made the decision to have a human experience, knowing that we are limited to those humanly senses. Along the way we got deluded and misdirected due to our perceptions, insisting on our free will and getting lost as we became more human. We lost our true selves and became more human than a spirit. We lost our sense of where we came from, what we are going through, and where we will end. Therefore, with some exceptions, most of our suffering is our own choice as our free will dictates. When we wake up from the illusion of this human experience, then we are ready to receive the presence of this higher power, higher intelligence, God. With that realization, we will then be rewarded with the knowledge that God was kind enough to grant us the journey, and grasp the fact that god has nothing to do with our suffering.

Love

> *What is this thing called love?*
> *We all want it*
> *Some fall into it*
> *Some look for it in all the wrong places*
> *Some don't realize they have it*
> *Some people buy it*
> *Some can't handle it*
> *We write songs about it*
> *So what does love have to do with anything?*
> —Casey

As discussed previously, love is merely a shared experience that allows us to connect to the core of every living thing. This is why we cannot give love—in reality we have nothing to give—but rather we can only share love with others. It radiates from our spiritual body and is a way to connect to our higher consciousness.

Most people spend their entire lives trying desperately to fill their emptiness with false love but end up living in a desperate world full of ever-deepening frustration and confusion, punctuated with brief positive moments. Our flawed beliefs, which are based upon what we were told or shown love to be in early life, lead us to constantly recreate unhappiness in our own lives.

Let's examine the difference between false love and real love.

False love

While unconditional love always exists, we are often unaware of it. Conditional love, such as parent-child love, dating, sexual love and romantic love, are the key roadblocks to real love. False love is momentary and feels wonderful; however, when it comes to experiencing true happiness, it falls short. Why is this? Why is conditional love unfulfilling, yet ready available in our world?

How would you feel if every time you cleaned your parents' house they told you they love you? After doing this for a few months or years, would you feel more loved? Of course not because the love was given with conditions. In fact, this kind of love is likely to lead to resentment. It is not a coincidence that people who do not have real love in their lives end up creating imitation love.

Once I went to the store to buy crab legs. Next to the crab legs there was a sign that said, "imitation crab." It looked just like the real crab but cost half the price. My curiosity got the best of me, so I asked the butcher if I could have a sample. As I took a bite, I asked him how it was made. He replied that it was made from a mixture of tofu and soy. Needless to say, I went home with the real thing. Sometimes there is no substitute for the real thing.

Without real love, we always feel the void. We always feel unfulfilled and insatiable. We can't seem to get enough sex, money, power, drugs, or relationships to satiate our need for love.

Real love/Unconditional Love

To love someone unconditionally means that you love the person exactly as they are, caring about the happiness of that person without any judgment and without seeking anything in return. We are really loved when other people care about our happiness unconditionally.

One of the very few times most of us have experienced unconditional love is soon after birth, when our parents most likely loved us unconditionally (assuming the pregnancy was wanted). But the love of parents for their children does not typically stay unconditional. Before long, conditions arise, and the message that "I won't love you unless . . ." is sent. In this way, love is judged against us; in turn, we end up judging ourselves as well as others for the rest of our lives.

Love is a problematic term on its own because of our misconceptions about our beliefs, perceptions, and feelings in early childhood. In early life, we were not able to differentiate between the behavior and the self. Hence, when we obeyed our parents' wishes like good little robots, we were rewarded with hugs and love. But they quickly vanished when we disappointed our parents. So the message was sent, "We love you as long as you are good," and the conditions were established.

As we grow, we establish our models of love in our subconscious mind without realizing that most of us inherited our parents' model of love and believed this to be the ultimate truth. Unconditional love is true love, while all of the other types of love are not real love. Couples in relationships, parents, and their children do not experience real love. Unfortunately, most of us do not experience unconditional love in our lifetimes, other than perhaps some occasional glimpses of it from time to time. This is why it is actually easier to experience unconditional love with a stranger than it is with someone close to us—there are no preexisting conditions or judgments. Although, even in this case, we still tend to quickly judge strangers based on our preexisting fears and beliefs.

Previously, we discussed the power of our beliefs, especially those of mistaken beliefs and how they dictate our lives. This also rings true when it comes to love. To truly understand love, and what true love really means to us, we must erase the old "tapes"—conditions under which we created our distorted views about love. This means learning to stop associating love with sex, marriage, relationships, and dating—only then are you ready to experience your highest self, and unconditional love. Then you have arrived.

Integrity

The integrity of the upright shall guide them, but the pervasiveness of transgressors shall destroy them.
—Proverbs 11:3

Does your word mean anything to you? Does what you say and do match? The word integrity is a derivative of two words; integritas, which means the putting on of armor, and integer, which means building a completeness, a wholeness. Throughout this book, I emphasize the importance of wholeness and the ways to achieve it. Integrity is an essential component of this process.

When we accept our physical body, our emotional body, and our spiritual body as our whole self, and that we do not need to be anything else but the reality of who we really are, we will at last experience complete self-acceptance. When we achieve the inner state that accepts that what we have is enough, our life takes on that wonderful proportion of balance and equilibrium. If we have integrity, it means that each part of us truthfully represents what we perceive, what we believe, and what we are. When we live our lives with integrity, we do not fear being found out because we have already found out who we are, are pleased with what we see, and have shown our true selves to the world.

Integrity is the keystone of all relationships. Integrity means what we say is what we mean and what we believe, and what we believe comes from an honest appraisal of the truth as we know it. Integrity is not being right all the time but recognizing with honesty and openness when we are not right. Integrity is taking responsibility for our lives and accepting and admitting the parts of our lives for which we have not taken responsibility. Integrity is not a perfect end state but rather a direction. It's an attempt to be the best that we can be and to hold ourselves to these standards. It's telling people exactly what we intend to tell them without fostering a posture to manipulate them into a more receptive position. We are not a salesman or an autocrat but simply a reporter, teacher, and a student. Integrity means we are willing to recognize the integrity of other people. Without giving others the right to their autonomy and freedom, our integrity is worthless because we are then saying "My integrity depends on having everything my way, having everything, period."

Integrity is the human soul in its highest form. It's an artist looking at the work upon which he has spent years and saying, "This is not my best. This is not ready yet." Integrity is the highest manifestation of self in our everyday world. When we live a life without integrity, we are constantly covering up; we see false things in other people, we have a negative outlook. We are suspicious of the other's actions because we do not believe in the sincerity of our own ways. We see our own actions as justified by their end, and we rationalize the means. One must have integrity at the beginning of the action; achieving the result is a reflection of that value system.

Your Purpose

> *A purposeless life is like,*
> *Day without the dawn and*
> *Night without the moon and the stars.*
>
> —Casey

Imagine you are in a raft and you are in rough water. You are tossing back and forth, feeling seasick, and wondering where the wind is going to take you. But you will make it safely to shore if you have the intent of making it. Your intention is the motive that carries you that chops through the waves. What you don't realize is that you are the one who is creating the wind—not some external force. You have determined the path and made it happen. If you are low on fuel, more than likely you are running in circles, not realizing you have been standing still, desperately waiting; trying to pretend you are not responsible.

The fact is that we chart our own course, and the work at hand is to get to where we are going while taking care of everything that needs to be done. In our family, that means if there is a problem with our children, parents, or spouse, we actively deal with it. That is the work at hand. This is our only course. If we sit in one place allowing the problems to get deeper and pretending nothing is happening, we will find ourselves falling further behind, feeling worthless about not doing what a good person needs to do to make things work.

A great life is a life without despair, without disillusionment. What happens to us is precisely what we have permitted to happen. We must be aware of our purpose. Each of our lives has a purpose, and the importance of embracing that purpose has to do with giving life the meaning it deserves. Our lives can mean something or mean nothing; either way the meaning it will have ultimately depends on how much we believe that we are going where we want to go, once we have decided we are a person worthy of getting what we deserve.

Ultimately, we are each our own therapist. No matter who we see, no matter what kind of medicine we take, no matter what kind of therapist we have, we are the ones who heal ourselves. No one gets us through grief but our own acceptance of the hurt and expressing the anger. The act of mourning, that is the relinquishing of the anger of coming to terms with ourselves, is the primary example of all healing. Since hurt is about suffering that loss, the act of being our own therapist comes with the understanding that we accept loss as real, and that we stop denying it and making excuses for it or pretending that it didn't matter. When we're faced with a loss, we need to allow ourselves to be with the hurt of the loss until the loss is gone.

In some way, the role of being honest with our feelings in everyday life allows us to come to terms with the feelings of this life. This enables us to be more and more honest about what we are feeling and to spend less energy trying to hold back our denied emotions.

Accept it. You are exactly where you are supposed to be in this life right now. Your life has gone exactly according to the way it was supposed to. You did what you did, and what happened is what happened because of it. Understand and accept all the forces of activity in your life. Plan with responsibility and grow. Know how feelings work by heart so you can resolve your toxic past. When negative emotions are allowed to persist, they become nothing more than a false experience that comes when your mind is unable to be free because you are holding to a pain that should not be there. Your thought process often takes detours suggested by unexpressed emotions. When you acknowledge that the negative emotion is false, you know that you are on the road to becoming free. It is easy to attain your purpose if you are willing to clean up the clutter of your mind, erase the false beliefs you inherited from your parents, allow your feelings and your intellect to complement one another. Only then can you tap into the guru within you. You need to make a decision for what is in your best interest, and you need to believe your best reality is not just a dream. Now that you attained the secrets of achieving your best self, you can create the best life for you by deciding that it is what you deserve and acting to make that deserved life happen.

APPENDIX A

Emotional Intelligence Test

All information contained in this Appendix is the property of I. Jerabek and K. McKenna and is used with permission.[51]

For decades, a lot of emphasis has been put on certain aspects of intelligence such as logical reasoning, math skills, spatial skills, understanding analogies, verbal skills, etc. Researchers were puzzled by the fact that while IQ could predict to a significant degree academic performance, and to some degree, professional and personal success, there was something missing in the equation. One of the major missing parts is emotional intelligence. For various reasons, and thanks to a wide range of abilities, people with high emotional intelligence tend to be more successful in life than those with lower EIQ even if their classical IQ is average.

EIQ test

Take the following test to determine your own emotional intelligence:

---

[5] Jerabek, I. & McKenna, K. (2006). What is your emotional IQ? (Abridged) PsychTests.com AIM Inc., http://testyourself.psychtests.com/testid/2091.

Read every statement carefully and circle the option that best represents how you feel. There may be some questions describing situations that you feel are not relevant. In such cases, select the answer you would most likely choose if you ever found yourself in similar circumstances.

1) If I have an uneasy feeling about a situation or a person, but cannot put my finger on what it is that bugs me, I just dismiss it and move on.

   a) Exactly like me

   b) A lot like me

   c) Somewhat like me

   d) A little like me

   e) Not at all like me

2) I keep myself up at night thinking about the problems in my life.

   a) Exactly like me

   b) A lot like me

   c) Somewhat like me

   d) A little like me

   e) Not at all like me

3) I have an urge to flee when someone gets emotional around me.

   a) Exactly like me

b) A lot like me

   c) Somewhat like me

   d) A little like me

   e) Not at all like me

4) I have difficulty snapping myself out of a grumpy mood.

   a) Exactly like me

   b) A lot like me

   c) Somewhat like me

   d) A little like me

   e) Not at all like me

5) I am impatient.

   a) Exactly like me

   b) A lot like me

   c) Somewhat like me

   d) A little like me

   e) Not at all like me

6) I find it hard to express my feelings to others.

   a) Exactly like me

   b) A lot like me

c) Somewhat like me

   d) A little like me

   e) Not at all like me

7) I adjust my behavior depending on who I am interacting with (e.g., calm and friendly with a child, serious and professional with my boss, etc.).

   a) Exactly like me

   b) A lot like me

   c) Somewhat like me

   d) A little like me

   e) Not at all like me

8) I get upset without really knowing who or what is bothering me.

   a) Exactly like me

   b) A lot like me

   c) Somewhat like me

   d) A little like me

   e) Not at all like me

9) The more difficult the challenge I face is . . .

   a) the more determined I am to succeed.

   b) the more I question my ability to succeed.

c) the more I get discouraged.

d) the more I feel like giving up.

10) How often do you find yourself going against your morals/principles, despite your better judgment? (e.g., letting a friend get away with something you know is wrong, turning a blind eye to an injustice, etc.).

   a) All the time

   b) Often

   c) Sometimes

   d) Rarely

   e) Never

11) Irene's friend is angry with her and Irene has no idea why. How do you think she should resolve the situation?

   a) Ignore him or her until he/she gets over it.

   b) Angrily demand an explanation.

   c) Calmly ask what's bothering him/her.

   d) Behave normally around this friend and hope that the issue blows over.

   e) Apologize for "whatever it is" that was done and hope that this friend forgives and forgets.

   f) I don't know.

12) Alex is preparing dinner when a friend calls in a panic. She is incredibly nervous about a job interview scheduled for the next day. She believes that she won't measure up to her potential employer's standards and worries that she will be humiliated. What would you do to help her feel more confident if you were Alex?

   a) Remind her of all the successes she has had in her life to help build up her confidence.

   b) Scoff at her concerns, and tell her that it's silly to be worried.

   c) Bring up some of her past failings in order to help her avoid repeating them.

   d) Tell her that her concern is understandable; the interview sounds really tough.

   e) Coach her through some strategies that were effective in past interviews.

   f) I don't know.

13) Patrick is meeting his partner, Eileen, at a restaurant after work. She is 45 minutes late, and when she finally arrives, she brings a friend from work with her. Nothing serious was holding her up—she and her friend simply lost track of time. Patrick is furious about being kept waiting. What do you think would be the best way to deal with this situation if you were Patrick?

   a) Take Eileen aside, vent my frustration, then rejoin her friend and try to have a good time.

   b) Lecture Eileen angrily in front of her friend.

c) Don't say anything but bring it up the next time Eileen makes me mad.

d) Make subtle remarks to Eileen throughout the meal (e.g., comment on how late they are finishing dinner) to let her know that I am not happy.

e) Leave the restaurant—I don't deserve this treatment.

f) Ignore Eileen as much as I can throughout the night to teach her a lesson.

g) Try to forget about it. Eileen is there now, and it's not worth getting mad about.

h) Bring it up when we get home and tell her that I would appreciate an apology or at least a phone call next time.

i) I don't know.

14) Amelia is struggling with her job she's been unhappy for a long time. She would quit, but her salary is great in comparison to most jobs she's had, and she is worried about finding work in an uncertain economy. She's feeling extremely depressed about her situation. What is the best thing to do to help with Amelia's unhappiness with her job?

a) Talk to her boss to find a way to make her current job more tolerable.

b) Quit her job immediately before things get worse.

c) Look for another job.

d) Do nothing and hope that things will eventually get better.

e) Deliberately sabotage herself at work (working inefficiently or being careless) until she is fired.

f) I don't know.

15) Andrew and his partner break up after a long, codependent relationship, and he's devastated. That chapter of his life is completely over without the chance of reconciliation. If Andrew were to come to you for advice on how to deal with his sadness, what would recommend?

   a) Stay at home and keep to himself until he recovers.

   b) Get busy—fill his days with activities that keep his mind and body occupied.

   c) Go over the events of the breakup in his mind over and over to make sense of what happened.

   d) Look to the future and try to use what he learned from the relationship.

   e) Focus on being happy on his own—enjoy the time he has to himself.

   f) Try to get back together with his ex at any cost.

   g) Seek the help of a therapist.

   h) Find someone new to date as quickly as possible.

   i) I don't know.

16) Erik is over at his parent's house for a dinner party. There are several other guests, some he knows and others whom he has just met for the first time. During the meal, his mother says something about his table manners that he interprets as a real put-down. He feels really embarrassed since everybody heard. What should Erik do in response?

   a) Suggest to his mother in a very calm tone that such remarks are uncalled for. He should smile to take any "bite" out of his comment and openly ask her not to say those types of things. In return, he should offer to make an effort to adjust his manners.

b) Nothing, despite his hurt feelings. It would be impolite.

c) He should point out some of his mother's most obvious shortcomings and point out that in today's world, no one really follows table etiquette anymore.

d) He should purposely eat more sloppily and forgo any table etiquette just to further embarrass her.

e) He should smile and say something to the effect of, "I learned all I know from you, Mom!"

f) He should make a scene at the dinner table, yelling at her about how rude she is and letting her know that he won't put up with comments like that. Then he should leave the table. Let her deal with the embarrassing silence—now she knows what it's like to be humiliated in front of other people.

g) Nothing. He should just smile and enjoy the meal. He shouldn't let his mother's comments about his table manners bother him—especially if she's right! He should mention to his mother after the guests leave or when they have a moment alone that her remarks made him uncomfortable. He should acknowledge that his table manners were perhaps not perfect but would have preferred if his mother had told him more discreetly.

17) One of Rowan's close friends is going through a very trying time. He has just had major surgery and needs a lot of help around the home for the next several months during his recovery. Rowan has been gladly pitching in several times a week with housecleaning, grocery shopping, and laundry duties. But lately, the demands have been getting to be a bit more than she can bear. She is feeling overworked and

underappreciated. As time goes by, her friend seems to only become more demanding! How should Rowan address the issue?

a) She should swallow her feelings of injustice and just do what he demands. He really needs her help after all, and he'd probably do the same for her.

b) She should just stop helping him.

c) She should mention to her friend that she is feeling pretty harried trying to take care of two households at once. She should still continue to come by to help out, but ask him to cut her some slack.

d) She should continue doing the housework, but not as flawlessly as she would do her own . . . maybe it will save her some energy when it comes time to doing her chores at home.

e) She should tell her friend about all the chores that have been neglected at her home, explaining that she just can't keep up with his demands. She should emphasize that he can either accept whatever she does manage to do for him, or find someone else.

f) She should explain that she has her own housekeeping to catch up on but would like to establish a schedule that works for both of them.

18) Alice's manager is continually dumping tasks on her desk. They are tasks that have to be completed before morning, and he always plops them down near the end of the day. The tasks are not her responsibility, but she has been helping him out without complaint for several weeks. She has been patient with her manager when he explains why he can't take care of it himself, but this has become a regular occurrence. What should Alice do?

a) Discuss permanently taking over the responsibilities from her manager in exchange for a raise, a promotion, or extra vacation days.

b) Bring up the issue with her boss. If he comes up with a good explanation, she should just agree with him and drop her complaints.

c) Threaten to quit or to get the union or HR involved.

d) Continue doing the extra work but intentionally make mistakes that will make the manager look bad.

e) Tell her manager that the extra work is really inconveniencing her because she's struggling to complete her own tasks and even has to stay late sometimes to finish them.

f) Nothing. He's her manager—she has no right to confront him or question his decision.

g) Just do what she can to complete them to the best of her ability—it's not likely that this will go on forever.

h) Tell her manager that she is happy to help out with the extra work—if he agrees to give the tasks to her at the beginning of the day and accepts that she will finish them after she completes her own tasks.

19) If someone were feeling enraged, which of the following activities would probably be the most challenging for him/her to do with ease?

a) Read a book.

b) Drive.

c) Console a child who is scared.

d) Exercise.

e) I don't know.

20) If someone were feeling sad, which of the following activities would probably be the most challenging for him/her to do with ease?

   a) Listen to music.

   b) Decorate the house for the holidays.

   c) Cheer up a friend who isn't doing well.

   d) Calling someone up to give them well wishes (e.g., birthday, before leaving on a trip, etc.).

   e) I don't know.

Scoring

Add up all your points according to this scoring chart:

Question	a	b	c	d	e	f	g	h	i
1	0	2	5	8	10				
2	0	2	5	8	10				
3	0	2	5	8	10				
4	0	2	5	8	10				
5	0	2	5	8	10				
6	0	2	5	8	10				
7	10	8	5	2	0				
8	0	2	5	8	10				
9	10	5	1	0					
10	0	2	5	8	10				
11	1	0	10	5	6	0			
12	10	5	0	3	10	0			
13	5	0	2	0	3	0	7	10	0
14	10	0	8	0	0	0			
15	0	5	0	10	10	0	10	0	0
16	5	2	0	0	5	0	8	10	
17	0	0	7	0	4	10			
18	7	3	0	0	8	0	1	10	
19	8	5	10	0	0				
20	0	7	10	5	0				

About emotional intelligence

In the late 1990s, emotional intelligence (EIQ) was one of the most talked about topics in contemporary psychology. In the business world, it became a hot topic largely due to one author's claim that a high EIQ was one of the best predictors of success in the workplace. In his 1995 book, Emotional Intelligence, Why It Can Matter More than IQ, author Daniel Goleman used an early definition by researcher Peter Salovey which stated that the construct of EIQ includes knowing one's emotions, emotional self-control, motivation and persistence, recognizing emotions of others, and successfully handling relationships. Goleman made some very strong statements in his book, including the suggestion that EIQ is one of the main keys to success in life. He implied that emotional intelligence is at the root of many of life's puzzles. Why are some smart people unsuccessful? Why do certain individuals strike out at others in a violent manner? Why so some excel at managing others while others struggle? He hinted that EIQ was an answer to all these, and many others, of life's questions.

Results

0-66

Your score on this assessment is not very strong. This is a concern because this test was designed to flag those individuals who might have limitations in understanding their own emotions and those of others. This area can certainly be improved with effort; however, for some people, it is difficult to improve without help. Seeking guidance from a professional (psychologist, psychiatrist, social worker, etc.) would probably be a great start to improving. On a positive note, awareness is key to helping you find the motivation to improve in this area and knowing which areas you most need to work on developing. By learning and practicing new skills and more effective ways of dealing with people, you can significantly improve your EIQ. The benefits will be numerous, including stronger relationships, a more successful career, better health, and personal happiness.

67-133

Your score on this assessment is reasonably good, but there is some room for improvement. Overall, you are fairly skilled at understanding and dealing with emotions. This is likely evident in your ability to relate to others, express your needs, and maintain a satisfactory level of emotional health. Since your score is in the mid-range however, you are not taking full advantage of your potential. Emotionally intelligent people have an easy time overcoming difficulties in their lives, and they are generally able to control their moods. It's easy for them to motivate themselves to overcome obstacles and reach their goals. In addition, they find social interactions to be quite easy and fulfilling for several reasons. They are comfortable allowing themselves to get close with others and feel comfortable being vulnerable enough to establish intimacy. They also report having an easy time offering support to others, likely due to an empathetic nature and a solid ability to offer advice.

134-200

Your score on this assessment is excellent. This means that you are able to express your feelings clearly in appropriate situations and are comfortable dealing with other people's emotions as well, which form the basis of your ability to relate to the emotions of others as well as well as your ability to understand yourself. Your emotions are your guide. You use them as a means to direct your judgment and reasoning in order to take appropriate action in emotionally charged situations. You are likely someone who owns your emotions, positive and negative. Not only does your ability to deal with emotions benefit and enhance your ability to create intimidate relationships with others, but it also allows you to better understand yourself.

INDEX

A

acceptance, 12, 120
  emotional, 33
anger, 52, 74-76
  effects on health of, 21
  feeling of, 37
anxiety, 62-63
  attacks, 65-67, 82
  curbing, 68-69
  projected, 64-65, 67-68, 121

B

being
  core elements of, 16
beliefs, 131-34, 136-37, 146-49
brain, 138-39
  development, 30

C

change
  resistance to, 109
compassion, 24, 80
conscious mind, 140
control, 65-66, 68, 72-73, 79

D

defenses, 108-9
depression, 53, 55, 86-87
discontentment, 60
Donchin, Emmanuel, 141

E

EIQ (emotional intelligence quotient), 159-70
EMDR (Eye Movement Desensitization and Reprocessing), 103
emotional body, 14, 16-17, 19-23, 25
emotional energy, 76, 121
emotional safety, 5, 34-35
emotional self mastery, 13-14, 41, 96
emotions, 20-21, 29-30, 41-44, 61, 67, 86, 109, 141, 171-72
energy, 21, 27

F

fear, 51, 62-63, 94, 115, 134
  of abandonment, 100
  of expressing feelings, 41

    in expressing the truth, 90
    of loneliness, 26
    of rejection, 36
    of social acceptance, 92
    of success, 64
feelings, 12-13, 31, 42-45, 51, 57, 98-99
    of anger, 37
    dealing with, 37
    defining, 50
    differences between emotions and, 41-43
    distractions for, 48
    failure to identify, 41
    gut, 6, 40, 95, 113, 121
    metaphor of the beach ball, 47-48
    negative, 36, 92-94, 115, 121, 127
    present, 120
    secondary reactive, 41
    six basic, 37, 40, 43-44, 49
    in the workplace, 90
Feelings Check, 44
Forgiveness, 6, 127-29

G

grief, 95
guilt, 53, 79-82

H

happiness, 50, 53, 58-61, 63-64
humility, 80
hurt, 52, 70-73, 75

I

integrity, 6, 153-55
intellectualization, 98, 102, 108
intelligence, 29, 96, 98, 159
intimacy, 111, 115-16, 172
intuition, 6, 29, 95-96, 139

K

knowledge, 13, 96, 99, 150

L

love, 25-27, 151-53

M

mind-body connection, 15, 42

P

pain, 70-71, 73, 75-77
perception, 133
physical body, 14-23
Psych-K, 103, 146-48
PTSD (post-traumatic stress disorder), 66
purpose, 24, 155

R

rage, 75, 77-79
Rand, Ayn, 13
reality, 12
relationships, 111-18, 126
remorse, 80
resentments, 115-16, 122-27

S

sadness, 22, 51-52, 69
safety, 34
self
  loss of, 71
self-acceptance, 34, 59, 80, 95, 154
self-conditioning, 66-67, 149
self-contentment, 40
self-criticism, 59
self-esteem, 33-34, 73-74
self-image, 33, 37, 59
self-worth, 73
shame, 20, 141-46

Socrates, 14, 146
spiritual body, 14, 16, 22-25
stress, 83-85
subconscious mind, 106, 113, 115, 134-35, 137, 140-41
success, 63-64

T

toxic shame, 142

W

Williams, Robert, 148

www.ingramcontent.com/pod-product-compliance
Lightning Source LLC
LaVergne TN
LVHW041840070526
838199LV00045BA/1358